Ethical Leadership
Creating and sustaining an ethical business culture

Andrew Leigh

KoganPage

LONDON PHILADELPHIA NEW DELHI

First published in Great Britain and the United States in 2013 by Kogan Page Limited

2nd Floor, 45 Gee Street
London EC1V 3RS
United Kingdom
www.koganpage.com

1518 Walnut Street, Suite 1100
Philadelphia PA 19102
USA

4737/23 Ansari Road
Daryaganj
New Delhi 110002
India

© Andrew Leigh, 2013

The right of Andrew Leigh to be identified as the author of this work has been asserted by him in accordance with the Copyright, Designs and Patents Act 1988.

ISBN   978 0 7494 6956 6
E-ISBN   978 0 7494 6957 3

British Library Cataloguing-in-Publication Data

A CIP record for this book is available from the British Library.

Library of Congress Cataloging-in-Publication Data

Leigh, Andrew.
    Ethical leadership : creating and sustaining an ethical business culture / Andrew Leigh.
        pages cm
    ISBN 978-0-7494-6956-6 (pbk.) – ISBN 978-0-7494-6957-3 (ebook)   1. Business ethics.
2. Organizational culture.   I. Title.
    HF5387.L45 2013
    174'.4–dc23
                                                                        2013020904

Typeset by Graphicraft Limited, Hong Kong
Printed and bound in India by Replika Press Pvt Ltd

*Ethical Leadership is dedicated to the memory of
my lifelong friend, the late Jim Greenfield*

CONTENTS

Introduction

If you eat meat but not fish, some people will call you a vegetarian. Others say you're not one unless you also avoid fish. Purists, though, will heap scorn on your claim to be one, unless you're a fully paid-up vegan. Running a responsible business and claiming to be ethical is rather like being a veggie. People differ about what being 'responsible' or 'ethical' actually means.

Faced with the seemingly impossible task of 'being ethical', some leaders stick to meeting legal requirements. For them, being ethical is easy – you stay strictly on the right side of the law. Yet avoiding only what is strictly illegal does not mean that what you are doing is right. In 2012, Lord Justice Leveson condemned the UK media for an 'unethical cultural indifference to the consequences of exposing private lives'. Intrusive behaviour by some newspapers was not illegal, only immoral.

In the worst dictatorships it may be technically legal to kill or harm certain individuals, but this won't make it morally right. Using child labour, mowing down rainforests or polluting your local environment may technically be within local laws. But sticking to the letter of the law may still mean that you are being highly unethical.

Running an ethical or responsible business is about developing your own moral compass – and ensuring that the company has a reliable one, too. Ethical leadership uses that moral compass to steer personal actions and the company's. You and your senior colleagues set the tone, and this is what leadership is ultimately all about. When Marks & Spencer decides its moral compass now includes a policy of sustainability, it does not create one for Next or Carphone Warehouse. When the Co-operative Bank takes an ethical stance about what investments to support, it too sets a tone, but it may not infect RBS or HSBC with the same rigour.

Any company wanting to set an ethical tone needs clear criteria for how it will judge its performance as a responsible organization. Starbucks, for example, has long claimed to set a tone regarding sustainability. It has scored commendably high in the listing of The World's Most Ethical (WME) Companies. Yet the criteria used do not include whether the company pays its fair share of local taxes – they are rapidly having a rethink about that!

There is a clear trend towards companies straining to be seen to be ethical. As James Ashton, City Editor of the London *Evening Standard* put it: 'Maybe it's the banks' tarnished images, BP's life after the Gulf of Mexico spill, G4S's Olympic high jump, tax-avoiding Amazon, or rip-off gas companies, but corporations seem more concerned than ever at getting it right in the eyes of shareholders, customers and governments'.[1] In the same week, expressing this point from a leadership perspective, Rich Ricci, then head of Barclays' corporate and investment bank stated: 'If I decided to stop trading soft agricultural products it is not driven by regulation, it is because it doesn't sit socially well with the large constituents of our customers.'

This apparent welcome conversion to ethical leadership understandably drew disbelief from the chairman of the parliamentary panel on corporate governance. Pointing out that reputation is now a competitive issue for banks, he questioned whether Barclays' declared position was merely 'a cynical attempt to gain more customers'.[2]

It almost certainly *was* an attempt to gain customers, which makes absolute commercial sense. Being ethical pays, as explained in more detail in Chapter 2. Even so, for every leader it poses a major personal challenge, since there are few absolute rules to follow. Relying on a tick-box approach does not work. The guiding principle therefore has to be:

> Trying to be ethical is better than not trying at all.

As a leader you must choose what ethical means to you and your company. Inevitably, some leaders avoid this issue entirely. Asked by the Leveson enquiry what interest he took in the ethical constraints of his newspapers, Richard Desmond, owner of the *Daily Express*, snorted: 'Well, ethical, I don't quite know what the word means.' Later the enquiry was shown a statement from him declaring: 'We don't talk about ethics or morals because it's a fine line and everybody's ethics are different.'[3]

It certainly is a fine line – which is why it requires not the abandonment of ethics and the wish to do the right thing, but genuine leadership, one that sets the tone for the entire company. It is also where your leadership character, integrity, authenticity and vision will be most severely tested and be put most publicly on display.

Risk

As Mr Desmond and others might wonder, what then does it mean to be an ethical leader? In trying to answer this for yourself and your company, several issues crowd in for attention:

- Why are ethics important for our organization?
- What drives unethical behaviour in our company – now and in the future?
- How will we establish and sustain an ethical business culture?
- Which of our business practices contribute to an ethical business culture?
- What leadership behaviours help create our ethical culture?
- How will we measure the effectiveness of programmes and policies designed to affect ethical behaviour?
- What risks do we run if we allow unethical behaviour to occur?

Each company must tackle these for itself, but throughout this book the answers will keep appearing. A common starting point is at least setting the goal of minimizing the legal risks for the company (see Figure 0.1).

If the goal is to reduce corporate risk in the purely legal sense, there have to be various observable outcomes: an increase in reporting on misconduct – unethical practices must be observed and acted upon; there must be less actual misconduct – employees behave more responsibly; and employees should feel safe reporting on ethical matters – they do not experience retaliation if they do so.

However, as will become clear throughout this book, sticking only to avoiding risks of breaking the law produces not an ethical culture, but a culture of compliance. By compelling or coercing people to behave as you want, you will not necessarily win their commitment, engagement or willingness to do what is necessary to do the right thing, such as speaking up when facing a potentially unethical action. This book explores what it takes to create a self-sustaining ethical culture, one which keeps building on its successes. There can be no single end-state labelled 'destination ethical culture', only an ongoing journey towards that constantly receding end point.

FIGURE 0.1   Minimizing the legal risks for the company

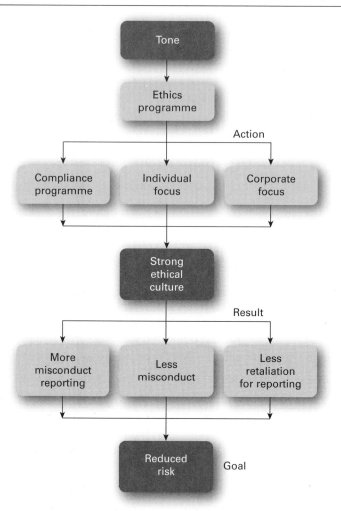

Dealing with the deluge

Pursuing an ethical culture is rather like walking one of those paths across moorland, where you can see where people have previously trekked. Yet it is still relatively easy to stray and get lost. We have been deluged in recent years with high-quality studies about ethical issues. Many show clearly what it means to be ethical in business, what an ethical company looks like, the advantages of being ethical, and the downside of allowing unethical behaviour to prevail. Numerous case studies of major corporations reveal that many take seriously the task of showing their stakeholders that they are being responsible members of the community. Equally, there are as many others dramatically revealing the price paid for allowing unethical behaviour to seriously damage company performance and reputation.

Making sense of this torrent of information and shared practice remains a problem. Much of the stuff is extraordinarily dense and hard to penetrate. This alone perhaps justifies the addition of *Ethical Leadership*, which attempts to synthesize and simplify. It tries to extract from the multitude of well-meaning studies and numerous case stories a workable resource for busy senior managers and leaders. This is why each main chapter starts with an Executive Summary – many readers may not have the personal space to read every chapter in full. It is also why each chapter concludes with action pointers – not rules or 'do this or do that', but rather signposts for the action-minded.

Are ethical leaders different?

In Liverpool's Walker Art Gallery, one of the most popular paintings is the famously titled *And when did you last see your father?* by William Frederick Yeames. We might ask the same about ethical leaders – when did you last see one? Do ethical leaders even exist? This is not an unreasonable question; close up, most senior executives appear flawed in some respect when it comes to running an ethical business. Yet contrary to the picture of leaders pervading the media, most executives want to be effective in their jobs and to leave their companies and the world a better place, creating value on both fronts for those whose lives they affect.

Apart from the blizzard of reports and academic papers on the subject of business ethics, what it means to be an ethical leader remains extraordinarily vague. Few leaders step out to declare proudly, 'I am an ethical leader', knowing that this is a hostage to fortune. For example, was the ex-CEO of Marks & Spencer more ethical than his fellow CEOs by introducing the M&S commitment to sustainability? Were the others less ethical because they had not?

Two important themes running throughout this book are the prevalence of ethical dilemmas in everyday business, and the role of leaders in shaping the company's ethical culture – their responsibility to set the tone.

Prevalence

Many executives and business thinkers believe that ethical leadership is either a mirage or merely about having good character. They argue that having 'the right values' or being a person of 'strong character' is enough. For them, the ethical leader will readily detect ethical dilemmas. He or she will set the example for others of withstanding any temptations that may occur along the way. While good character and the right values are certainly important, ethical leadership is more complex and the stakes are much higher.

To be an ethical leader is indeed to be different. This kind of leader acknowledges the complexity of running a responsible business, yet tries to do it anyway. 'Ethical leaders embody the purpose, vision, and values of the organization and of the constituents, within an understanding of ethical ideals. They connect the goals of the organization with that of the internal employees and external stakeholders.'[4]

Tone

Throughout the book you'll encounter numerous ways of becoming an ethical leader. The main message, though, is the importance of setting an ethical tone. This is all about shaping the culture and the company climate. No leader does this alone, yet equally tone starts at the top.

Setting the tone is a combination of practical actions, attitude and articulating values. Your ability and willingness to promote ethical conduct consistently is critical to ensuring that employees understand and engage in ethical decision making. The task is to use values to steer the organization towards a sustainable ethical culture. A leader who sets the tone for an organization will draw on personal values, things that matter most for them. William Rogers, CEO for the radio group UKRD which won the top spot in the Sunday Times 100 Best Companies two years running, shares what this can mean in practice: 'Building a values-based culture is hard work, but I believe that if the culture and values of a business are right, are followed and enthusiastically lived and breathed at all levels, all else being equal, the business will come right.'[5]

Shaping the culture is as much about understanding the emotional aspect of company activities as it is about setting up formal mechanisms to encourage desired behaviour. This is why the book explains first the organizational requirements for affecting culture and then a separate section focusing on the individual requirements. The two main charts which show the corporate and individual approaches to generating an ethical culture are repeated at the beginning of relevant chapters to provide a useful reminder of the context for each chapter.

Throughout the book you will encounter numerous ways to become an ethical leader, without suggesting that there is a single point of arrival. Instead it points to what will be required to shape the organization to have a sustainable ethical culture. Being an ethical leader really is about the journey and less about the destination.

Notes

1 Ashton, J (2012) Reputations on the line, *Evening Standard*, 29 November

2 Schäfer, D (2012) Barclays eyes crop trading retreat, 28 November, http://www.ft.com/cms/s/0/1145f7ec-397f-11e2-85d3-00144feabdc0.html#axzz2N9LDelmw
   In April 2013, Barclays announced the departure of Mr Ricci, who trade union officials said 'represented everything wrong with the banking industry in general'.

3 *Mirror* News, 3 July 2012

4 Freeman, E and Stewart, L (2006) Developing ethical leadership, Business Roundtable Institute for Corporate Ethics

5 Rogers, W (2012) Sound advice, *People Management*, August

PART ONE
Making sense of ethical leadership

Making sense of culture

01

EXECUTIVE SUMMARY

- Time spent on cultural issues is far more productive than any amount of strategic discussions and forward planning.

- Senior executives are more willing these days to talk publicly about culture.

- A study of over 200 companies found that those working on changing their culture improved revenue by over 500 per cent and stock prices by over 800 per cent.

- Culture now takes centre stage in many organizations.

- Aligning culture to strategy can create a language and route map for how to bring a leader's vision alive.

- When leaders invest their energies in culture, it can inspire a whole workforce.

- Though culture is a bit of an enigma, it's no excuse for ignoring it or giving it little attention.

- Culture is the personality of the organization and it's where values reveal themselves through behaviours, attitudes and decisions.

- A culture shift is often the only way a company can renew itself, find a fresh purpose or redirect its collective energies.

- To achieve a culture shift requires those leading it to avoid their own behavioural bias: inertia and natural resistance to change; everybody's doing it; overconfidence; halo effect; hero syndrome.

Mention culture and, until recently, you could expect managers to 'reach for their sick bags'.[1] For many of them, based not just in the UK but around the world, culture seemed excessively vague and frankly irrelevant. Yet there are encouraging signs that the sick bags are being replaced with yellow pads. On these appear careful calculations showing the extraordinary value of culture to the bottom line. Quite simply, culture is money.

Ignoring culture's potential to make a difference to company performance is therefore to wilfully bury one's head in the sand. Meanwhile others, often competitors, are busily figuring out how best to put it to profitable use.

In earlier decades, top executives devoted precious thinking time to working on strategy. Today, in the memorable aphorism of Merck's then CEO: 'Culture eats strategy for lunch!' Translating this into ordinary speak, time devoted to culture issues is far more productive than any amount of strategic discussions and forward planning.

As the same CEO elaborated: 'You can have a good strategy in place, but if you don't have the culture and the enabling systems that allow you to successfully implement that strategy, the culture of the organization will defeat the strategy.'[2] Yet for many organizations and those in senior positions, culture remains something of a 'hidden persuader' – a critical and underrated influence.

So what is changing? First, there is more awareness, among both executives and those who study organizations, of how it impacts on company success. For example, a detailed study by Professors John Kotter and James Heskett of Harvard Business School produced startling evidence that showed the extent to which focusing on culture makes a positive difference (see box below).

The cultural payoff

Quite simply, companies that pay attention to their culture outperform those that don't. The advantage of paying attention to more than just profits to stockholders can produce an enormous payoff.

In a study reported by John Kotter, a world expert on leadership, over an 11-year period, firms focusing on culture increased revenues by an average of 682 per cent, versus 166 per cent for the ones that did not.

Culture-minded companies expanded their workforces by 282 per cent while those less focused on culture only increased their workforce by 36 per cent. Similarly, the culture-minded companies grew their stock prices by 901 per cent versus 74 per cent for the non-focused companies. They also increased their net incomes by 756 per cent versus 1 per cent.

SOURCE: Kotter, J and Heskett, J (1992) *Corporate Culture and Performance*, Free Press, New York

Second, a bruising succession of corporate and even whole industry failures, such as the financial crisis of 2008, has involved unacceptable and reputation-destroying behaviours. This has triggered widespread demands for altering current cultures, along with questions about the best way of achieving this. Thirdly, and partly because of these failures, senior executives seem more willing to talk publicly about culture.

Talking about corporate culture is relatively easy. However, transforming one can be extremely challenging. Soon other priorities crowd in, shouldering aside the sustained efforts needed to affect change. Yet for those willing to stick with it, the metrics of culture offer an alluring prospect. For example, it can have a demonstrable impact on a commercial organization's bottom line. One 11-year study of just over 200 companies, for instance, found that those working on changing their culture improved revenue by a staggering 516 per cent, net income by a huge 755 per cent and their stock prices by a lucrative 827 per cent.[3] Fortune 100 Best Companies have similarly shown a higher return than the S&P 500 over seven years, with a positive relationship between a strong affirming culture and performance.[4] Nor is culture's positive impact restricted solely to financial return. It reaches far and wide, affecting risk, strategy, reputation, performance and customers.

When things go seriously wrong with how an organization, or even an entire industry, operates, urgent demands for culture change soon surface. Invariably, someone important emerges to talk of the inevitability of cultural transformation or to describe the intention to initiate significant change. For example, Mervyn King, then Bank of England Governor, perhaps stating the obvious, told members of parliament in August 2012: 'Barclays needs a new culture.'[5] And following the Libor scandal an independent director at RBS was tasked to conduct a significant 'review of the culture and values' of the bank.[6]

Apart from financial services, revelations of damaging behaviours have engulfed numerous society sectors in recent years. These have included the police, MPs and their expenses, certain pharmaceutical companies, engineering firms bribing their way to exports, and of course the media. Some have generated intense shock and dismay. Only the promise of cultural change and, in some cases, renewed ethical standards seems an acceptable form of response. For example, the UK media phone-hacking saga precipitated widespread demands for cultural and ethical change across an entire industry. And faced with the uphill struggle of reforming the culture at the *News of the World* and rescuing a soiled brand, its owners simply abandoned it as a lost cause, shutting down the paper. It was a sobering and expensive demonstration of the price of ignoring the role of culture in day-to-day management.

Culture now takes centre stage in many organizations because this is such a powerful way of making a positive difference. It influences, for example, whether people use their full potential and go the extra mile on behalf of the organization. By aligning culture to strategy, leaders can create a language and a route map for how they want to bring their version of the future alive. And when leaders invest their personal energies in building and pursuing a particular cultural approach, it can inspire an entire workforce.

What is culture?

On a day of slow business in the early 2000s, two traders at Merrill Lynch in New York undertook a bet: that neither could consume the entire contents of a vending machine. The rest of the trading floor ground to a halt. Everyone watched and wagered as the two traders gorged themselves to the point of sickness.[7] You would hardly expect this type of behaviour in the offices of a top management consultancy or a law firm. Apparently harmless, it was a vivid example of the prevailing culture associated with financial traders:

> Culture is not a fluffy chimera of business how-to books, or self congratulatory corporate reports. Culture, real and unnoticed as the air we breathe, is the web of unspoken, mutual understandings that frame what people expect from others and think is expected of them. (Chief executives must tend to the values of their companies, *Financial Times*, 20 August 2012)

Although managers and leaders now talk more openly about culture, it retains its rather mystical persona. Yet the enigma of culture is no excuse for ignoring it, or giving it short shrift. Louis Gerstner, the executive who rescued IBM from near oblivion, for example, admitted that previously he had regarded culture as among several important elements producing success. But while at IBM he came to see that 'culture isn't just one aspect of the game, it IS the game'.

Formal definitions of corporate culture might seem helpful, yet its very nature is so wide-ranging that these tend to confuse, rather than enlighten. For our purposes, perhaps the most accessible is: 'the way we do things around here'. Putting it slightly differently, culture defines the proper way to think, act and behave in an organization. Those who do things in the 'proper' way will fit in, and can become quite successful. Those who choose not to do things in the proper way do not last with an organization. They are told: 'We don't do things like that here.'

In essence, culture is the personality of the organization. Above all, it's where values reveal themselves through people's behaviours, attitudes and decisions. We make sense of culture through values and things associated with them (see Figure 1.1).[8] Values can be positive or destructive. For example, positive values include trust, openness, creativity, honesty, integrity and care. Damaging values might include power, blame, greed, status, being liked and so on.

FIGURE 1.1   Recognizing culture

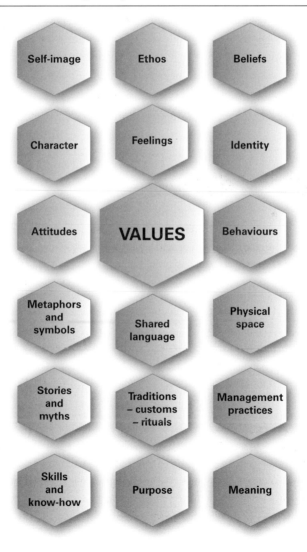

Perhaps unhappy with something as simple as 'the way we do things around here', anthropologists have tried to pin down culture more precisely. They see it as a body of learned beliefs, traditions and guides for behaviour shared among members of a group.[9] This somewhat esoteric explanation would probably not last long in most organizations. Instead, a useful extension of the workable 'the way we do things round here' is that each person in an organization IS the culture.

Culture shifts

It is hardly surprising that even the best leaders approach the prospect of attempting cultural shifts with considerable caution, even reluctance. After all, around half to two-thirds of all major corporate change initiatives fail and less than 40 per cent of change efforts produce positive change.[10] Most people realize that it is going to be a marathon, not a sprint.

Yet in many situations a culture shift is often the only way that a company can renew itself, find a fresh purpose or redirect its collective energies.

Three examples of a cultural shift

Marks & Spencer

M&S set itself the goal of putting sustainability at the heart of the company's long-established culture. Its Plan A evolved into the aim of becoming the world's most sustainable major retailer. Launched in January 2007, it began with 100 commitments to achieve in 5 years and has since been extended to a further 180 commitments to achieve by 2015.

This significant culture shift requires M&S to 'work with our customers and suppliers to combat climate change, reduce waste, use sustainable raw materials, trade ethically, and help our customers to lead healthier lifestyles'.[11]

Sears Roebuck and Company

The US retail company radically changed how it did business and dramatically improved its financial results. Its culture shift involved a new Total Performance Indicator – a set of measures showing how well the company was doing with customers, employees and investors. The shift also meant that every individual in the company learned to use a tool for self-assessment and self-improvement.[12]

Procter & Gamble

In 2000, P&G had a culture of 'not invented here'. The CEO appointed that year needed to shift the culture to one where innovation reflected deep understanding of customers' needs and perceptions. Innovation needed to accelerate dramatically. It could only be done if the entire organization embraced new ways of working.

P&G now required a culture of trust and open exchange across the entire organization and with key external players. The workforce had to make fundamental changes: increased focus on the customer, greater curiosity and openness to new ideas, and much more internal and external collaboration.

The prevailing culture was successfully shifted from 'not invented here' to 'proudly found elsewhere'. Organization structures, systems, communications and even recruitment reinforced the new culture and desired behaviours. All this effort closed the gap between old thinking and the new innovation-driven strategy. From this significant culture change sales doubled, profits quadrupled, and the company's market value increased by more than $100bn.[13]

Two key factors to take into account in considering whether to even attempt to affect a company's culture are: the strength of the existing culture and special features unique to a particular organization.

Strength of existing culture

The stronger the culture, the harder it will be to replace it, or even to nudge it along a new path. To recognize a strong culture, ask those involved why they have chosen to work for the organization and what they care most about it. With a strong corporate culture you are likely to hear consistent answers, reflecting shared purpose and values. In Boeing, for instance, asked what he did for the organization, a cleaner famously replied 'I'm helping to build a new airplane', while his equivalent in NASA answered 'I'm helping to put a man on the moon'.

In contrast, weak organizational cultures may put up less resistance to change while also allowing strong subcultures to emerge. When this occurs, people's attention can switch to entirely the wrong things; behaviours may even turn toxic. A recent example is the money-laundering breaches at HSBC's Mexico offices, involving millions of dollars for drug cartels. An almost total disconnect emerged between what those at the head office in

London saw as the company's culture and those working in Mexico. Despite the cultural divide there was no remedial action until far too late. When cultures are weak or irrelevant they also make it harder to manage well, leading at best to inefficiencies and at worst to dishonest behaviours.

A strong corporate culture offers a clear vision of what the organization is about and where it is going. This is underpinned by corporate values; these are both consistent with the aims of the company and employees feeling that they also reflect or are aligned with their personal values. Such a culture usually values its people highly and there is considerable employee interaction across many levels. It is also adaptable, adjusting to external conditions, and consistent, treating all employees equally and fairly.

Special features of the culture, unique to a particular organization

What can make changing culture so challenging is that every organization has its own unique version – even within the same industry. Consider, for example, the cultures of Ryanair and British Airways and how different it would be working for, or being a customer of, either. An identikit formula for creating a culture shift in both would almost certainly not work. Likewise, even though Waitrose regularly compares its prices to Tesco's, the two operate very different cultures, right down to how they lay out their stores and talk to their customers and staff.

In the early 2000s the US health-care company Aetna was struggling to deal with a variety of problems. The situation was exacerbated by a mainly irrelevant culture that encouraged people to be risk aversive, tolerant of mediocrity and suspicious of outsiders.

The prevailing executive mind set was 'we take care of our people for life, as long as they show up every day and don't cause trouble'. Attempts to tackle this unsatisfactory set-up were made worse by a merger with a lower-cost health provider, resulting in a serious culture clash.

A new management team tackled the turnaround without ever describing their efforts as culture change. They simply began with a few small but significant behavioural changes that helped revise the culture while preserving its strengths.[14]

Shifting culture starts with defining how things should be, even if they are not like that yet. It means understanding the perceptions, judgements, attitudes and feelings of the workforce, since without this you are flying blind. These understandings are as important in shaping actual new behaviours as any formal mechanism. It may be harder to make sense of assumptions, unwritten rules, rituals, personal goals, and feelings that develop over time than the formal, visible elements of corporate culture. Yet there are ways to analyse these less tangible components and to set up formal mechanisms to make positive change happen.

Another way of gaining insight into a possible culture shift is discovering how that culture was formed. For example, it can mean trying to understand how employee attitudes and perceptions were created in the first place. Taking time to unravel what gets employees fired up is an important way of creating a dedicated powerhouse moving the organization forward towards its strategic goals.

Avoiding the rocks

Given that the route to a successful shift in culture is strewn with rocks, some more like huge boulders, what are the biggest ones to watch out for? The largest are to do with your own behaviour in how you tackle the journey and can be summed up as trying to avoid behavioural bias.

Behavioural bias 1: Inertia and natural resistance to change

If you have to push a heavy weight, it doesn't mean that it cannot be moved. But to push it you had better work out how to move it – where to put the lever to shift the weight. Inertia and resistance are part of the laws of physics. Yet they are also relevant when it comes to change in people and organizations. People tend to resist change, but some tend to resist more than others.

Attempts to shift a corporate culture significantly will usually involve changes in how everyone behaves on a daily basis. The scale of the change breeds its own problems, providing plenty of scope for inertia to exert its deathly grip or to galvanize resistance.

A deeply embedded culture is particularly tough to shift and understandably leaders may delay attempts to change it, viewing such actions as literally a last resort. Others may regard change as easy, a foregone conclusion, while failing to establish a sufficient sense of urgency. Consequently there is a danger that events will overtake them. By then, culture may have turned into an excuse and a diversion.

Excuses often given for not implementing or pursuing a culture shift include:

- It's all too complicated and difficult.
- How do I know the best approach to adopt?
- Things are alright as they are now.
- What if I go ahead and it all goes wrong?
- I don't have time to plan something this fundamental – I've enough daily pressures to deal with.

It is worth watching out for these kinds of delaying tactics since they have the potential to stop any worthwhile change in its tracks.

Behavioural bias 2: Everybody's doing it

In April 2012, the price of silver hit its highest price in decades, having achieved a meteoric 500+ percentage increase since late 2008. 'At one point or another,' comments an experienced investor, 'a little voice in my head and many others watching this rise kept saying "You have to get in now, this is a golden opportunity!"'

Then came the inevitable crash and the price plummeted a staggering 32 per cent in just one week. The investment lesson was about herd mentality. When everyone else is piling in and results seem too good to be true, that's when it is time to get out or avoid getting into a particular investment.[15]

Also, have you ever noticed that when you cross a busy road, as well as clocking the traffic, you subconsciously follow what your neighbours do? Scientists have recently put a figure on this and worked out that we're 2.5 times more likely to cross if our immediate neighbour makes a move to cross.[16]

The above lessons apply just as much to culture shifts. Just because you keep reading or hearing about them does not mean that your own organization automatically needs one. Many attempts to alter culture happen simply because others are already doing it.

For some companies a culture shift is the least desirable choice when facing immediate problems and challenges. For example, a sustained effort to reduce overheads may be far more effective than attempting a long-term culture shift that could take between 5 and 10 years to be fully embedded and producing a payback.

Yet it's a fact of life that companies are now paying far more attention to culture and its impact.

Behavioural bias 3: Overconfidence

Thomas Watson Jr, the founder of IBM, is supposed to have said around 1943: 'I think there is a world market for maybe five computers.' Not only was he wrong, but he probably never even said it. But Cambridge mathematician Professor Douglas Hartree did say, around 1951: 'No one else would ever need machines of their own, or would be able to afford to buy them.' Wrong!

Most car drivers, for example, believe that they are above average in skill compared to other people. Clearly this is impossible. Cognitive psychology shows how we tend to be overconfident about beliefs and abilities. We also tend to be naturally optimistic about our assessment of the future.

In the same way, those embracing culture shift may tend to feel that they have a good grasp of the issues and are likely to succeed. As mentioned earlier, the record of failed change efforts says otherwise.

Practical experience of introducing culture shifts suggests that the safest way to start is by acquiring an awareness of what you are getting into. Do you really understand the risks you may be running?

Behavioural bias 4: Halo effect

Have you got a proud record of achieving several short-term change efforts? If so, you may feel that a cultural shift will not be significantly different from what you did previously. This particular rock along the way is similar to the one labelled overconfidence we met earlier. Feeling that you have special change-management skills allowing you to tackle a culture shift may be just that – a feeling.

Previous experience of successfully managing short-term change in an organization encourages the illusion that a long-term culture shift will be equally predictable. This particular bias also explains why many investors buy stocks when prices are rising on the grounds that they are likely to continue doing so.

Behavioural bias 5: Hero syndrome

Culture change is sexy. It's high-profile stuff and a sure way of putting your stamp on the business. It's the equivalent of sweet, fatty food. That is, while it's highly attractive it can also be bad for your health, or in this case your career. It can be tempting to start a culture shift for entirely the wrong reasons – raising your personal profile. Along the way, for example, you pull all kinds of organizational levers: make public pronouncements, take centre stage at town hall meetings, conduct media appearances and generate a satisfying amount of attention to your every word internally.

Finding yourself engaged in attempting a culture shift for the wrong reasons can be a personal disaster, as well as bad for the organization you work for. Make sure you have thought through why you want a culture shift and have properly assessed the risks of pursuing it.

Assessing your culture

Ask your doctor for a complete health check and the first question might be: 'Are you worried about your heart, cancer, lung problems, fitness or what?' If you shrug and say 'Everything!' you will probably be sent to a specialist centre where they conduct scores of different tests. It will take hours, if not days of your time.

Likewise, if you are going to attempt to shift the culture it makes sense to know your starting point – what is the culture right now? While there are many ways to assess your company's culture, the starting point needs to be some problem or issue. For example, Johnson & Johnson decided to survey employees about how the company was doing relative to its Credo, which described the ethical expectations of the company. Apart from specific results about customers and safety which were a special concern of top management, the findings were seen as a way of keeping the ethical code alive.[17]

Diagnosing culture for its own sake is too vast a problem and the results will probably be costly, boring and useless. Assuming you have a specific problem you want to address, for example 'we believe that people are not always acting ethically or following our core values', a cultural survey could make sense.

However, there are many so-called surveys out there all claiming to measure culture. So how will you decide which to use? One might tell you how flexible your organization is, another might identify specific ethical problems, and yet another may measure something exotic, like the extent to which people are willing to relate to each other. Not only do you probably not know what questions to ask, but you risk measuring only superficial aspects of the culture. Survey instruments seldom go really deep to dig out the tacit assumptions of the culture. Also, there are probably subcultures within the company which can royally confuse the final assessment. Think how hard it is to analyse your own personality with all its many layers. Organizational cultures, too, have multiple layers to unravel.

Despite these difficulties, it is possible to assess the culture with reasonable accuracy for helping to design your eventual cultural shift. It may take external professional help to steer the process and will probably involve diagnostic sessions with various groups within the company. If you want to know how ethical your culture is, consider using the approach developed for the World's Most Ethical Companies annual survey. This uses a well-structured questionnaire based on five basic variables that contribute to an ethical culture.[18]

ACTION POINTERS

- Don't resent time spent on culture – it is likely to be more useful than strategy discussions or forward planning.

- Assume that each person in your organization IS the culture.

- Choose a culture shift to help the company renew itself or find a fresh purpose, or redirect its collective energies.

- Avoid attempting a culture shift as a way to raise your own profile within the company.

- It's important, in attempting a culture shift, to take into account the strength of the existing culture.

- Consider any unique features of your organization that might affect the effort to alter the culture.

- In attempting a culture shift, define how things should be, even if they are not like that yet.

- As a way of gaining insight into the culture, discover how it was formed.

Notes

1 Stern, S (2007) Wake up and smell the coffee on your corporate culture, *Financial Times*, 27 March

2 Weeks, J (2008) An unpopular corporate culture, IMD International, September

3 Heskett, J and Kotter, J (2011) *Corporate Culture and Performance*, The Free Press, New York

4 Great Place to Work Institute and Frank Russell Company (2005), quoted in above fact sheet

5 Chief executives must tend to the value of their companies, *Financial Times*, 20 August 2012

6 Banks have hit a new low, RBS Chief admits, *Guardian*, 4 August 2012

7 Getting to grips with finance's culture problems, *Financial News*, 15 August 2012

8 See also Schein, E (2010) *Organizational Culture and Leadership*, Jossey Bass, San Francisco – Schein's list representing culture includes additional concepts such as group norms and habits of thinking.

9 Bennett, RA (1984) *Culture and Conduct: An excursion in anthropology*, Wadsworth, Belmont, CA

10 Gilley, A (2005) *The Manager As Change Leader*, Praeger, Westport, CT

11 Plan A, Doing the Right Thing – see for example M&S Corporate Publications (2010) Plan A Commitments 2010–2015

12 The employee-customer-profit chain at Sears, *Harvard Business Review*, online, 5 March 2009

13 Why people do what they do: demystifying corporate culture (2011), HR Review, Analysis of HR Strategy and Practice, Home Page, Leader, 19 September

14 Katzenbach, J *et al* (2012) Culture change that sticks, *Harvard Business Review*, July–August

15 Miller, GE (2011) Silver selloff highlights dangers in following the herd when investing, 20somethingfinance.com, 9 May

16 The risks of following the herd, and banded mongooses (2010) Planet Earth Online, 12 October

17 Treviño, L and Nelson, K (2011) *Managing Business Ethics: Straight talk about how to do it right*, 5th edn, John Wiley & Sons, Inc, Hoboken, NJ

18 See www.ethisphere.com/worlds-most-ethical-companies-faqs/

The ethical advantage:
What's in it for your organization?

02

EXECUTIVE SUMMARY

- There is seldom anything entirely obvious about ethical choices within companies, or in creating an ethical culture.

- Ethics are about the rules of behaviour or 'doing the right and ethical thing round here'.

- More specifically, ethics are a standard of conduct for what is good or bad, right or wrong, acceptable or unacceptable.

- There is now strong evidence that pursuing an ethical culture is associated with business success.

- To affect your culture you will need to get beneath the skin of ethics.

- This means understanding some of the important implications of developing a corporate moral conscience: behaviour driven by *compliance*, by *social conscience* and by *moral principles*.

- Only moral principles will ensure that your people take ethical decisions by relying on internally driven values.

- Going deeper into ethics will allow senior staff to consider more fully what it means to create an ethical culture and provide a common language for talking about the issue.

In 2012, the Church of England had a revelation. In a Damascene moment, its money minders finally got the message. News Corp had no intention of reforming its corporate governance. After the phone-hacking scandal and with much soul searching, the Church investors realized that it could no longer ethically hold the company's stock. They sold its shares.[1]

Meanwhile, Maynard Leigh Associates wondered whether it should continue doing business with News Corp, which regularly hired its venue for staff development sessions. We began asking ourselves a challenging ethical question. Where did our company stand in dealing with an organization which, in many people's opinion, had endorsed or turned a blind eye to criminal behaviour?

E-mails flew around the company as people shared their often strongly held views. Some argued that this was business we could ill afford to reject. Others, equally concerned, quoted our core value of integrity. They argued that it was incompatible with continuing the existing commercial relationship. The company's leadership was split. In fact, our ethical position was rather less clear than some of us thought.

Similarly, a huge debate occurred within the Royal Shakespeare Company about whether to continue accepting sponsorship from BP given its poor environmental credentials.[2] So split was the RSC that it even allowed an 'alternative Shakespeare Company' to perform briefly on its stage before regular performances. The interlopers delivered an amusing but scathing skit on BP's environmental credentials. They urged the audience to tear the BP sponsorship logo from their recently purchased programmes.

Close up, views of right and wrong, what matters and what does not, what is ethical and what is not, turn out to be surprisingly varied and often not at all easy to resolve. For example, it is seldom as simple as 'Telling lies to your manager is wrong.' Ethical choices pose genuine dilemmas: Is the only way to win the order to pay a sweetener? What do we do about a supplier suspected of using child labour? Do we ship these products to meet a deadline, despite knowing that they're possibly faulty, or do we discuss the difficulties with the customer? Do we delay payments to suppliers when our cash flow is severely limited?

In resolving such dilemmas, company ethics never stand in splendid isolation. They are an intrinsic part of the company's broader culture. We can best sum them up as the rules of good behaviour, or even more colloquially as:

Doing the right and ethical things around here.

Certainly this version is over-simplistic and the section on page 36 on 'dissecting ethics' further unpicks this admittedly tricky concept. Yet in practice, the above phrase works as a handy expression of what an ethical culture means. Despite its apparent vagueness, people seem to understand the loose phrasing. However, inevitably it provokes further questions, such as: How do we start strengthening our ethical culture? What do you mean by 'doing what's right'? What does ethical mean? Who is to say what's right? How do we tell if doing something is wrong? What happens if we don't do what's right? What are the rules we should follow?

> For millennia, people have argued about ethics or the rules of human conduct. These 'moral principles' governing the behaviour of groups or individuals are always highly debatable and often charged with emotion.
>
> *Ultimately, ethics means: a standard of conduct for what is good and bad, right and wrong, acceptable or not acceptable.*

Some specific benefits of an ethical culture

'The debate is over' for many people who ask: 'What does an ethical culture mean for daily business?'[3] The issue is no longer 'Do we need an ethical culture' but 'How do we create one?' Whether you explore the impact on customers, the effect on a company's share price or the reduction in reputational risk, ethical cultures offer real benefits to companies and indeed individual performance.

Let's get specific. First, customers admire and prefer dealing with companies choosing to put ethics at the centre of their culture. It begins to establish a hard-to-copy competitive advantage, including a strong public image. Between 1994 and 2000, Bucharest was not a great place to hire a taxi. Not that there was a shortage, there were thousands. But when you got one, the meter would run at random speed, if at all. At journey's end you would have to negotiate, sometimes violently, with the driver to agree on the fare. Then one day a taxi company started charging based only on a fair and honest meter reading – it attracted so much business that it caused all other taxi companies to start operating in this way.[4]

In 1992, the Co-operative Bank in the UK asked its customers why they banked with it. Most replied that they did so because it was an ethical bank. This shocked the Co-operative Bank, as it had no formal ethical policy and did not regard itself as particularly ethical. It had gained the reputation because it was one of the few UK high street banks with no direct relationship with apartheid South Africa.

The bank decided that if its customers used it because they liked this approach, it was sensible to adopt a formal ethical policy. Subsequently the bank's commercial lending increased from £571m in 1992 to £4.4bn in 2008: an annualized growth rate of 14 per cent. This was despite rejecting £1bn worth of business as breaching the bank's ethical principles, for example because of a firm's involvement in fossil fuel extraction, the arms trade, animal testing, engagement in financial practices regarded as unsound, or connection with oppressive governments.

In one consultation exercise on its ethical policy, 80,000 customers responded. The bank also experienced continued growth during the global banking crisis – in contrast with most of its competitors. Ethics are remarkably good for business. The main reason for acting ethically is that it's the right thing to do, although people certainly differ over what that means in practice.

Second, most employees actually prefer earning less working for an ethical company than being paid more and working for an unethical company. So by building its ethical profile your company will tend to lower the normal cost of staff attrition, while retaining valuable talent. It's definitely worth having.

Third, more than one in three people at work say they have left a job because they have disagreed with the company's ethical standards.[5] Build your company's ethical culture and you start creating a reputation that goes beyond retaining talent and starts attracting it.

Fourth, because employees like working in an ethical culture and commit to its values, this helps create an early warning system. This becomes a natural insurance policy against employee misconduct and reduces the chances of expensive litigation or punitive action.

Fifth, ethical cultures create strong affirming places to work. They do this by encouraging a commitment to strong teamwork and productivity. For example, research into Fortune 100 Best Companies to Work For found a positive relationship between a strong affirming culture and individual and corporate performance.[6] Putting it slightly differently, by spending time on cultural issues companies start to reap the rewards of better performance than competitors. There is nothing vague or insubstantial about such gains. For example, the strength of a company's ethical culture drives: 1) whether or not employees feel pressure to compromise company standards; 2) the rate of observed misconduct; 3) whether employees who observe misconduct choose to report it; and 4) whether those who report feel retaliated against.[7]

Recognizing an ethical company

So what does an ethical company look like? How would you recognize one if you came across it during your travels? Healthy ethical cultures have zero tolerance for destructive behaviours such as incivility, aggression, sexual harassment, and discrimination. You also know that a healthy culture exists if the organization uses shared values, codes of ethics, and continuous ethical improvement.

More specifically, the recently established World's Most Ethical (WME) Companies Index uses five measurable aspects of a company's activity, each accounting for a proportion of an ethical culture (Table 2.1).

TABLE 2.1   Elements of an ethical company (%)

Ethics and compliance programme	25
Reputation, leadership and innovation	20
Governance	10
Corporate citizenship and responsibility	25
Culture of ethics	20
Total	100

SOURCE: World's Most Ethical Companies methodology, 2012. Ethisphere. Reproduced with permission

The WME Index is extremely detailed, asking such questions as when was the company's ethical code last updated, or is there a written plan for training employees in ethical issues. Reflecting best practices around the world, a company with an ethical culture would reveal:

- Employees with a sense of responsibility and accountability for their actions and for the actions of others.
- Employees feel free to raise ethical issues and concerns, without fear of retaliation.
- Managers and leaders model the behaviour they demand of others.
- Managers communicate the importance of integrity when making difficult decisions.

- Leadership understands the pressures that drive unethical behaviour.
- Leadership develops processes to identify and remedy those areas where pressures occur.

Similarly, the Ethical Resource Center (ERC) uses some 27 criteria for deciding whether a company has a weak or strong ethical culture. These include misrepresenting financial records, environmental violations, insider trading, illegal political contributions, anti-competitive practices and so on.[8]

While these data can help us get to grips with what it means to be an ethical company, they only take us so far. For instance, the metrics produced by the WME methodology and the criteria used by the ERC ignore some of the wider issues which can affect a company's ethical reputation. For example, Starbucks appears as one of the world's most ethical companies. Yet a Reuter's investigation showed that the company generated £398m in UK sales in 2011 but paid no corporation tax. As MP and tax campaigner Michael Meacher put it, Starbucks' practice was 'profoundly against the interests of the countries where they operate and is extremely unfair. They are trying to play the taxman, game him. It is disgraceful.' Not long after this onslaught from lawmakers, tax campaigners and the media, the company announced that it was considering changes to its UK tax practices.[9]

Staying clear of trouble: avoiding risk

A powerful and persuasive reason for acting ethically is to avoid running unacceptable risks and costs, such as being fined, sued or even in rare cases causing death. Strong ethical cultures reduce observed misconduct, lower the pressure for people to act irresponsibly and encourage less retaliation for reporting unethical behaviour (Figure 2.1).

Serious unethical behaviour can completely destroy a company. There is already an excess of real-life examples of this happening, including Enron, WorldCom, Arthur Andersen, *News of the World* and many others. Not all firms die, though, as a result of ethical failures. Many absorb their punishment and move on, feebler perhaps but still functioning. HSBC, for example, was significantly weakened when in November 2012 it warned that money-laundering fines could top $1.5bn while additional costs from mis-selling ran into more millions. Despite this, the bank seemed likely to survive but the full costs are likely to be undetected and underestimated.[10]

Unethical behaviour may not kill a company. But when its behaviour becomes known, as inevitably it will in the age of the internet, it can reduce

FIGURE 2.1   Strong co-worker culture reduces observations of financial misconduct

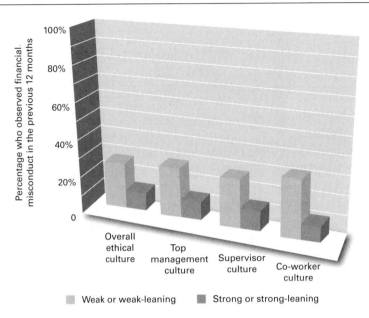

Weak or weak-leaning   Strong or strong-leaning

access to capital markets, drive down stock prices and force the firm to pay a premium for loans and debt financing. Steady growth in the use of ethical criteria by institutional investors means that lapses in corporate social responsibility can rapidly dent a plc's share price, or a private firm's prospects of finding investment.

An accurate picture of the full costs of potential ethical failures is often hard to obtain, yet they are real. Despite this, such costs are often entirely absent from company annual reports, the balance sheets or the income statements. Figure 2.2 describes the potential business costs of ethics failures on three levels. Some, particularly those at higher levels, are chronically undervalued in executive decision making. This is usually due to a lack of leadership knowledge and common reasoning errors.

Level 1 costs of ethical failure are fairly easy to calculate and rapidly gain leadership and management attention. Level 2 costs stem mainly from the bureaucratic nature of the business and it is hard to tie these costs directly to ethical failures. However, leaders almost certainly underestimate their size. Finally, level 3 costs are the hardest to quantify and include such things as customer defection, reputation loss, moral loss and employee cynicism.

FIGURE 2.2   Executive decisions and the business costs of ethical failures

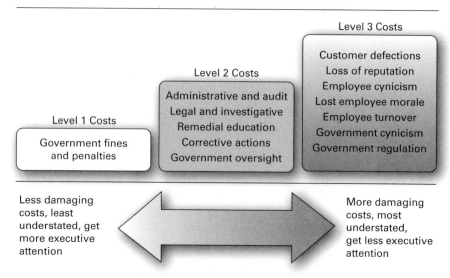

Level 3 Costs

Customer defections
Loss of reputation
Employee cynicism
Lost employee morale
Employee turnover
Government cynicism
Government regulation

Level 2 Costs

Administrative and audit
Legal and investigative
Remedial education
Corrective actions
Government oversight

Level 1 Costs

Government fines
and penalties

Less damaging costs, least understated, get more executive attention

More damaging costs, most understated, get less executive attention

SOURCE: Thomas, T *et al* (2004) Strategic leadership of ethical behaviour in business, *Academy of Management Executive*, **18** (2). Reproduced with permission

Third, employees like working for ethical companies, with various benefits to their companies as a result. For example, in stronger cultures, far fewer employees (4 per cent) feel pressure to commit misconduct than in weaker cultures (18 per cent).[11] Similarly, the costs of retention and recruitment tend to be significantly favourable compared to less ethical firms.

However, the most persuasive argument for running an ethical business is simply that it is more profitable. There is a strong financial case for running companies in an ethically responsible way and, even in a recession, investing in ethics benefits a company.[12] The earlier-mentioned World's Most Ethical (WME) Companies label applies to companies that truly go beyond making statements about doing business 'ethically' and translate those words into measurable action. WME companies demonstrate real and sustained ethical leadership, along with impressive profits. Figure 2.3 compares the World's Most Ethical Companies against the S&P 500 since the setting up of the WME Index in 2007.

Statistical purists may demand yet more proof of an actual causal relationship between ethics and profits. But for the rest of us, the evidence is as convincing as any other normal business metric describing company performance: 'The truth is that companies that have the ethical advantage demonstrate better financial performance than companies that don't.'[13] Or

FIGURE 2.3 Percent returns: World's Most Ethical Companies vs S&P 500

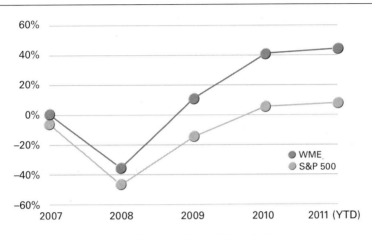

SOURCE: World's Most Ethical Companies. Reproduced with permission

as the normally hard-nosed profession of accountancy puts it, after an in-depth study of building ethics into strategy: 'Once they have adopted an ethical approach, companies will often find there are bottom line benefits from demonstrating high ethical standards.'[14]

Too good to ignore

Around the world, businesses are designing and implementing business ethics programmes and not just because of legal pressures. Astute organizations increasingly realize that they must address issues of ethics, social responsibility, and the environment.

Addressing these in a systematic way helps firms improve their own business performance. In particular, the effort can expand opportunities for growth and contribute to the development of their social contacts and networks. More specifically, there are business benefits such as:

- enhanced reputations and goodwill;
- reduced risks and costs;
- protection from their own employees and agents;
- stronger competitive positions;
- expanded access to capital, credit and foreign investment;
- increased profits;

- sustained long-term growth;
- international respect for enterprises and emerging markets.

Enterprises that excel in these areas create a climate of excellence for their employees, shareholders, and communities, and contribute to the economic well-being of their countries.[15]

Just how much it pays to be ethical is particularly hard to answer. However, a study by the *Wall Street Journal* in 2012 explored this issue by looking at what consumers were prepared to pay for two basic commodities: t-shirts and coffee. The conclusion was: 'In all of our tests, consumers were willing to pay a slight premium for the ethically made goods. But they went much further in the other direction: They would buy unethically made products only at a steep discount.'

Also, companies don't necessarily need to go all-out with social responsibility to win over consumers. If a company invests in even a small degree of ethical production, buyers will reward it just as much as a company that goes much further in its efforts. 'Companies should therefore make a particular effort to reach out to buyers with high ethical standards, because those are the customers who can deliver the biggest potential profits on ethically produced goods.'[16]

Companies earning the most revenues have the most to lose from ignoring ethical considerations. Therefore they tend to work the hardest at building strong ethical cultures.

Equally, to maintain their strong performance they face unique pressures that could drive up the level of misconduct in their workplaces. Yet in a major national study of business ethics, misconduct soared from 48 per cent of companies with a strong management commitment to ethics, to 89 per cent where management commitment was weakest.[17]

Putting this result slightly differently, successful companies know that it pays to look after the culture and make sure it stays ethical. As one of Denmark's long-lasting successful companies puts it: 'Danfoss lives up to the expectations of being a responsible world citizen. This is deeply rooted in our history and culture and it is reflected in the way we carry out our daily business.'

Or: 'The Board of Airport Commissioners and Los Angeles World Airports are committed to the highest standards of ethical business conduct and aim to treat in an ethical manner those to whom we have obligations, including the City of Los Angeles, employees, tenants, customers, suppliers and neighbors. LAWA shall conduct its business not only in accordance with all applicable rules of law, regulations, policies, procedures and guidelines, but with the highest of ethical values.'

Why values matter

Values run deep in the human psyche. They lie at the heart of the organization and its ethical culture. For that reason alone, they can be challenging for any company to consider. Begin talking about values and other issues soon surface, such as: How can we know that our corporate values are ethical? What happens if someone behaves against the values? How much personal commitment will these take? It soon becomes clear that the route to an ethical culture is not an instant one.

Consequently, in many places the task of building an ethical culture descends into destructive short-termism, as the Chartered Institute of Management Accountants explains:

> Businesses can be tempted to make short-term gains by turning a blind eye to ethics. Despite codes of practice, regulatory oversight and ever-increasing public pressure, many firms routinely ignore ethical considerations. Some even claim that a business simply needs to abide by the law without concerning itself with broader ethical issues. Yet such disregard can undermine the wider economy and, in time, cause irreparable damage. Lessons must be learned from the corporate collapses of the past decade: myopic strategies can create massively profitable entities, yet impressive initial results may turn out to be unsustainable. (CIMA)[18]

Companies stuck with short-termism tend to go through the motions rather than attempting a real culture shift. One cause stems from the impatience of investors. Half a century ago, they would hold UK or US shares for an average of about seven years. Now it's less than seven months. Since a culture makeover can take far longer, this may be unwelcome news.

A survey of chief financial officers of over 400 companies found that to meet their quarterly earnings numbers, three out four of them would reject investment projects that only enhanced the long-term value of their firms.[19] Of the more than 1,700 executives polled by Ernst & Young for its annual fraud survey, 15 per cent said that they were prepared to make cash payments to win business, up from 9 per cent in the previous survey; 47 per cent of the 400 chief financial officers surveyed felt that they could justify potentially unethical practices to help business survive during an economic downturn.

SOURCE: Survey finds unethical business practices on the rise, *Wall Street Journal*, 23 May 2012

So for many organizations and their leaders, the prospect of creating an ethical culture seems to lack pace, agility, or the appeal of reasonably rapid results. Without these, though, it can be hard to win board approval to take ethics activity seriously. Instead, some choose to massage the language. For example, they may rephrase what's needed into 'changing the organization's climate' or 'achieving behavioural change'. Or as one leading systems company puts it, in a phrase redolent of its mechanistic approach, 'to energize the market units'. These do not alter the reality that moving towards an ethical culture will normally demand a marathon, not a sprint.

Your organization will only move towards an ethical culture if it understands the full range of values and behaviours needed to meet its ethical goals (Table 2.2). This requires people to be fully engaged with the organization's purpose, which in turn drives ethical behaviour.

TABLE 2.2   Values and ethics

Business values	Ethical values
Customer service	Integrity
Customer service/relationships	Honesty
Quality	Openness
Innovation	Respect
Reliability	Fairness
Efficiency	No waste
Value for money	Responsibility

Making sense of ethics

When Leonardo da Vinci wanted to draw human beings better, he could have just given himself endless practice. No doubt he would have improved. But he also took to dissecting corpses. Beneath the human skin, he realized, lay all kinds of mysteries of the skeleton, muscles, veins and internal organs. Leonardo was given dead bodies by a hospital and dissected 30, carefully drawing many of the parts. His depiction of bones and muscles were to help other artists to paint the human body properly.

Ethics pose a similar challenge for leaders and managers. How do you get beneath the skin of ethics to help your organization make moral choices and guide its behaviour? According to CIPD research, for example: 'There is a current disconnect between business values and the personal values of employees.'[20] One approach is to see your ethical organization as made of different layers, in which certain values are encouraged and others discouraged. For example, the basic need is for an environment in which employees feel physically and emotionally safe to report unethical behaviour and to do the right thing, and with systems and processes supporting that (Figure 2.4).

FIGURE 2.4   The layers of an ethical organization

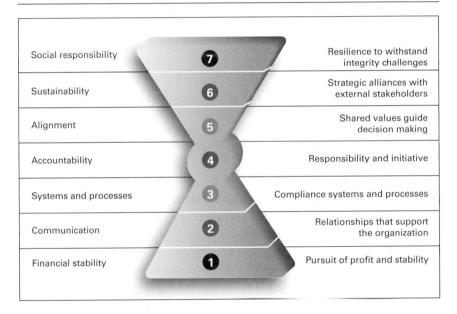

Social responsibility	**7**	Resilience to withstand integrity challenges
Sustainability	**6**	Strategic alliances with external stakeholders
Alignment	**5**	Shared values guide decision making
Accountability	**4**	Responsibility and initiative
Systems and processes	**3**	Compliance systems and processes
Communication	**2**	Relationships that support the organization
Financial stability	**1**	Pursuit of profit and stability

SOURCE: Gebler, D (2005) *Is Your Culture a Risk Factor? Using culture risk assessments to measure the effectiveness of ethics and compliance*, Working Values Ltd. Reproduced with permission

These different layers are stages along the way towards a corporate moral conscience. At the most basic level:

> *Compliance drives behaviour* – this is best summed up as 'Remember the rules and do what they say'. Some managers and leaders decide to end their journey right here. Get the rules right, goes their reasoning, and we've surely cracked the ethical issue for our organization.

The trouble is that compliance takes you only a short way towards the final destination of a corporate moral conscience. If people merely do as you tell them, they will seldom take responsibility for the lives they lead, or what happens at work. This is the opposite of what you need in journeying towards an ethical culture.

One of the most famous cases of behaviour driven by internal rules of compliance was the Ford Pinto case in 1971. Ford was, in effect, operating a management principle that crudely said that all difficult management decisions could be resolved using cost–benefit analysis – not much else mattered. It proved to be truly disastrous for the company.

Ford engineers discovered that the Pinto's fuel tank was a serious safety risk. Under certain circumstances – for instance, rear-end collision – it could explode, killing the occupants, who would most likely burn to death. Did the engineers tell their boss about this problem? 'Hell no!' said one of them working on the Pinto. 'That person would have been fired. Safety was not a popular subject around Ford.'

So they duly conducted a cost–benefit analysis. This numbers exercise compared the cost likely to arise from the company facing litigation and compensation claims, against the 'cost' or value of a human life. Side by side, the figures seemed a no-brainer. Even though the cost of rectifying the fault was a mere $11 per car and would save 140 lives per year, it was still technically 'cheaper' to do nothing and, instead, pay out occasional court-awarded damages for compensation.

However, the analysis took no account of social conscience. Nor did it refer to what should have been the firm's moral compass. The human and emotional circumstances behind the numbers never figured in the calculations. Quite simply, Ford failed to do the grown-up moral thing.

Apart from far larger than expected court damages, the decision cost Ford serious, long-term reputational damage. Also, how do you think Ford employees felt once the court cases began and their company was publicly accused of 'reckless homicide' – only dismissed by the courts much later?

It was also a vivid demonstration of how ethics – or lack of them – can affect the bottom line, and how a company can lose its moral compass (see page 40).[21]

The second level along the way to a corporate moral conscience is:

Social conscience drives behaviour – this is best summed up as 'Doing what's right is doing what's best for others'. In our own lives this implies friendship and altruism. We don't just think of ourselves, we are also concerned with the welfare of others. In a company this implies developing empathy for others, understanding how to interact with them to produce the best result for everyone.

The limitation of social conscience is the many difficult questions it raises about whether something is always right and what is best for everyone. No wonder managers and leaders struggle with this aspect of ethical culture.

An example of behaviour driven by social conscience is when a company decides to respond sympathetically to employees suffering from some form of addiction. Alcohol abuse and drug problems cost billions in absenteeism, workplace accidents, errors in judgement, and even embezzlement or theft to feed addictions. Some studies indicate that nearly 10 per cent of the working-age population has some sort of substance-abuse problem.

Yet when it comes to treatment for addictions, many employers and insurers shy away from lending a helping hand – from doing the right thing driven by social conscience. Instead, firing employees for drug addiction – breaking the rules – may seem like the answer. But it is only a temporary fix. The company must advertise for new employees, then absorb the cost and time to train new employees, and production slows as a result. The new employee may leave or not work out in the long run, therefore wasting the time and money that went into replacement.

More and more companies are therefore developing their social conscience and providing employees with treatment. Not only is it socially caring, but the actual cost is far less than may be expected. It helps the company, the employee and the community as a whole. In return the company gets an employee who already knows the job and comes back being more productive than before. There are fewer absences and far fewer injuries.

The final stop along the way towards a corporate moral conscience is:

Principles drive behaviour – this is grown-up ethics and best summed up as being virtuous or acting with integrity. It's having a moral compass (Figure 2.5). For example, in your company it might mean encouraging desirable behaviour such as acting with courage, fairness, honesty, consistency, openness, transparency, self-discipline, sustainability and so on. Or it could mean recalling faulty products well before anyone else notices they are defective.

FIGURE 2.5   The moral compass

A moral compass means that doing what's right stems from within, not a set of written rules, or an interaction with others. Instead, the 'right' action comes from beliefs or values.

It is sometimes hard for each of us to know our own moral compass, let alone what the company one looks like. Take, for example, the decision of Maynard Leigh not to do business with tobacco companies. As a company whose mission is Unlocking People's Potential, we did not want to deal with people who were hell-bent on harming other human beings, albeit under the guise of giving them a certain kind of pleasure from smoking. That decision was relatively easy.

But how should we respond when a major defence contractor calls offering a juicy contract? That tested not so much our compliance behaviour – following a set of rules – as our social conscience and moral principles. From the experience we learned to judge each case on its merits. You cannot simply say 'we won't work for any defence contractor on the grounds that such organizations are all hell-bent on killing people', as this is patently untrue.

Stock market value versus doing the right thing

What should your company do if you discover that something's gone wrong with one of its products, putting the public at risk? A sound moral compass tells you that it's sensible to take action sooner rather than later. Yet immediately recalling the product could damage brand equity, spoil consumers' quality perceptions, tarnish the company's reputation and lead to both revenue and market share losses.

Worse, the stock market seems to regard a proactive strategy, such as an early product recall, as a signal of impending serious financial losses. Consequently, proactive strategies may have a more negative effect on a firm's value than more passive ones.[22] Knowing this, would you still recall the product and be active about doing so? This is when the corporation's moral compass may experience a head-on crash with reality.

Until recently, companies have chosen to steer by the North Pole Star of maximizing shareholder wealth. This compass point has driven some to make socially and morally questionable decisions. As Steven Denning, author, ex-World Bank executive and experienced financial commentator bluntly puts it: 'Maximizing shareholder value is a powerful idea. It is simple. It is elegant. It is intuitive. It has at least one big problem: it doesn't work.'[23] Others, too, have arrived at this conclusion:[24] 'This is a tragically flawed premise, and it is time we abandoned it and made the shift to a third era: customer-driven capitalism.'[25]

Ninety-five per cent of shareholder value is driven not by company performance, but by shareholders' expectations. These can be and often are manipulated. Executives with stock options have great incentive to massage results to manage investor expectations.

A company driven by values and a strong moral compass accepts the verdict of Wall Street but does it anyway.

What use are these rather fine distinctions of ethical behaviour – behaviour driven by compliance, social conscience and moral principles? Can they really help your company move towards a more ethical culture? Tests have been developed to assist people get to grips with these different ethical criteria. However, their main benefit lies in providing a way of going deeper into the whole issue of understanding and planning shifts in the ethical culture. They provide a common language and a way of making sense of the choices for action.[26]

ACTION POINTERS

- Develop your own clear statement of what you mean by ethics. For example, you might explain that you're talking about the rules of good behaviour within the company.

- Consider adopting the more colloquial phrase '*Doing the right and ethical things around here*' – or create your own easily understandable statement.

- To clarify what an ethical culture really means for your organization, make the personal decision to commit quality time to the issue.

- Values lie at the heart of an ethical culture. Therefore, spend time getting yourself and your colleagues clear about what values really matter to you and the organization – if necessary, reduce these to a few simple-to-understand words.

- To win the commitment of others, you may need to find a way of expressing ethics and values in ways that they can more readily understand. However, do not hide the fact that installing an ethical culture may take more than a few months or even a year of effort.

- Become familiar with some of the nuances of ethical behaviour and be ready to talk about behaviour governed by *compliance*, by *social responsibility* and by *moral principles*. Have some examples up your sleeve to help concretize these concepts.

- Be ready to talk about the company developing its moral compass and why that's important. Explain that a moral compass means that people do what's right by drawing on strongly held values, not a set of written rules.

Notes

1 Kuchlet, H (2012) Church sells stake in News Corp, *Financial Times*, 8 August

2 Cooper, C (2012) All the world's a stage, *The Independent*, 3 October

3 See, for example, Heskett, J and Kotter, J (2011) *Corporate Culture and Performance*, The Free Press, New York

4 Garner, J (2011) Leading with integrity, Tomorrow's Value Lecture Series, 19 October

5 Treviño, L and Nelson, K (2011) *Managing Business Ethics*, John Wiley & Sons, Inc, Hoboken, NJ

6 Great Place to Work Institute (2005)

7 Ethics Research Center (2009) National Business Ethics Survey, Supplementary research brief

8 Ethics Research Center (2009) National Business Ethics Survey, The importance of ethical culture

9 Bergin, T (2012) Special Report: How Starbucks avoids UK taxes, Reuters, 15 October

10 Thomas, T *et al* (2004) Strategic leadership of ethical behaviour in business, *Academy of Management Journal*, **18** (2)

11 See Note 8 above.

12 CIMA (2010) Incorporating ethics into strategy: developing sustainable business models

13 Mitchel, J (2001) The ethical advantage: why ethical leadership is good for business, Center for Ethical Business Cultures

14 See Note 3 above.

15 US Department of Commerce (2004) Business ethics: a manual for managing a responsible business enterprise in emerging market economies, Washington, DC

16 Trudel, R and Cotte, J (2012) Does being ethical pay? *Wall Street Journal European Edition*, 19 June

17 Ethics Resource Center (2012) National Business Ethics Survey of Fortune 500 employees

18 See Note 3 above.

19 Haldane, A (2012) The dangers of haste, *Prospect Magazine*, September

20 Employees not recognizing business values (2012) HR review, Strategy and Practice, 6 November

21 See, for example, Leggett, C (1999) The Ford Pinto case, www.wfu.edu/~palmitar/Law&Valuation/Papers/1999/Leggett-pinto.html

22 Chen, Y *et al* (2009) Does a firm's product-recall strategy affect its financial value? *Journal of Marketing*, 73, November, 214–26

23 Denning, S (2012) Is the tyranny of shareholder value finally ending? *Forbes*, 29 August

24 Why maximizing shareholder value is a flawed goal (2012) B2B Organic Growth Newsletter, Jan–Feb

25 Martin, R (2012) The age of customer capitalism, *Harvard Business Review*, January

26 Steare, R and Stamboulides, P (2008) Who's doing the right thing? *ethicability* ® *Moral DNA Report 2008*, Roger Steare Consulting Limited.

Towards an ethical culture

03

EXECUTIVE SUMMARY

- Be aware of the influential myths about ethical cultures and how you might deal with them. There's an explanation of seven significant ones.
- Some important benefits of having an ethical culture include:
  - Customers prefer dealing with companies who put ethics at the centre of their culture.
  - Most employees would prefer to earn less working for an ethical company than being paid more and working for an unethical company.
  - More than one in three people at work say they've left a job because they've disagreed with the company's ethical standards.[1]
  - If you adopt an early warning system against misconduct it reduces the risk of you facing expensive litigation.
  - An ethical culture helps make your company a strong affirming place to work in.
- The foundations of an ethical culture include values, attitudes, meaning, behaviours, purpose, and management practices.
- The chapter draws particular attention to the significance of formal and informal leadership and management practices.
- There's a list of key questions if you decide to conduct an ethics audit.
- A three-step starting point for tackling a shift towards a more ethical culture is: understand the nature of ethics; develop a unique plan of action; be values driven.
- The chapter has a useful framework for tackling change – it's like a contour map for tackling the desired shift.

If you can develop an ethical culture, it's literally money in the bank. The positive impact on the bottom line can be extraordinary. Once established, it can deliver the kind of sustained competitive advantage that many companies will come to envy. Like anything worthwhile in life, though, to reach such a culture can be demanding work.

The reverse is also true. If your corporate culture ignores ethical issues you may well increasingly pay a high price for this neglect. It may take the form of heavy fines, reputational damage and even criminal prosecutions. Sounds an exaggeration? Not really. Bribery and corruption, for instance, is the second leading reason for unlawful activities in Western companies.[2]

Ethical businesses are not a new phenomenon, of course. During the industrial revolution many companies in the United States and Europe thrived on a strong philanthropic tradition. What is new is the way ethics now need to be seen as a core part of companies' strategies and how they are being embedded into management culture at all levels.

Adopting an ethical culture might seem to be common sense. For example, the new CEO appointed to clean up Barclays' act was publicly declaring, within two weeks of his appointment, that ethical behaviour would from now on become a bank priority.[3]

What exactly does an ethical culture look like? What are the visible identifiers that an organization has an ethical culture? Based on both research and a general overview of what is admittedly a vast landscape of facts and opinion, the main features are:

- Ethical leadership – leaders set the right tone at the top and model ethical culture as part of earning the trust of employees. Leaders can be trusted to do the right thing.

- Supervisor reinforcement – employees look to immediate supervisors for signs that the tone at the top is important and is taken seriously. Individuals directly above the employee in the company hierarchy set a good example and encourage ethical behaviour.

- Peer commitment – peers talk about the importance of ethics and support one another in 'doing the right thing'.

- Embedded ethical values – a sense of 'how we do things around here' is integrated into daily activities. Values promoted through informal communications channels are complementary and consistent with a company's official values.

- There are formal rules and structures to govern and guide stakeholders in pursuing an ethical business approach, plus a system to oversee and monitor compliance.

Myths that can undermine the culture

But various myths may conspire to undermine even the best leaders' willingness to move towards an ethical culture. They usually arise from misunderstandings and difficulties that previous leaders have experienced in trying to traverse this admittedly tricky terrain. Let's look at seven of them squarely in the face, to see how they might relate to your own organization.[4]

Myth no 1: It's easy to be ethical

Some people believe ethics are easy: you just apply the 'smell test' and if something stinks, don't do it. Or would you be proud to tell your mum about some action you are taking? In other words, if one wants to be ethical it's easy; it doesn't need to be managed.

This myth ignores the complexity surrounding ethical decision making, particularly within business organizations. Ethical decisions are seldom simple. For example, people often do not automatically know that they are facing an ethical choice. They simply do not recognize that there is a moral choice involved. Few problems come along waving a red flag saying: 'I'm an ethical issue, you had better think about me in terms of morality.' This is why organizations often spend precious time training their people in how to become aware of an ethical issue.

Most adults therefore look outside of themselves for guidance on ethical situations, either by referring to supervisors and line managers, or by reference to society's rules and laws. Again, what this means in practice is that most people need to be led when it comes to ethics.[5]

Myth no 2: Business ethics are more about religion than management or leadership

Behind this myth lies the confused belief that ethics are a means of altering people's values, changing them as people and even undermining their fundamental beliefs. The reality is different. An ethical culture deals with managing values between the individual and the company. It's simply a systematic way to handle the inevitable conflicts that crop up in every business on a daily basis.

How far do people in your organization regard ethics as relevant to what the company does? For instance, what's the reaction when you mention ethics or the idea of a corporate moral conscience, or talk about 'our moral compass'? Watch the expressions. Listen for the verbal reaction. There's work to do in dispelling this damaging myth if you conclude that people seem to view ethics as almost 'out of bounds'.

Myth no 3: Our employees are ethical so we needn't waste time on business ethics

Know this myth for what it really is. It's actually an excuse for avoiding action. All organizations face complex choices, many involving conflicts between competing interests. For example, when a customer mistakenly overpays, how quickly do you reimburse them? Do your employees feel confident about dealing with ethical dilemmas? Is there a tendency to refer to 'honesty' as a catch-all for ethical choices, which on closer examination are more complex than merely not doing something illegal?

Deal with this myth by giving people plenty of real-life examples of ethical dilemmas faced in daily life at work.

Myth no 4: Best leave business ethics to philosophers, academics and priests

Be patient with this reaction when raising the issue of ethics in your company. It tells you just how far back some of your colleagues are in understanding the whole issue. They simply do not yet appreciate its total relevance to your current organization and need your help to get to grips with change.

This myth is a favourite cop-out as it ignores the reality that business ethics is a discipline. It is nonsense to suggest that this stuff is only suited to mystics and the less worldly. Deal with this myth by sharing with colleagues some of the highly practical tools for making sense of the issue – such as ethical audits, codes, risk reduction strategies, targeted training and leadership guidance.

One of the best ways to kill off this particular myth is to help people understand why the issue poses daily dilemmas for people, such as reporting behaviour which could put everyone's job at risk. The demise of Barings Bank might have been avoided in 1995 if colleagues had been more confident in expressing their concerns about the unauthorized trading by its head derivatives trader in Singapore. Instead, as the subsequently jailed trader claimed: 'People at the London end of Barings were all so know-all that nobody dared ask a stupid question in case they looked silly in front of everyone else.'[6]

Myth no 5: Ethics can't be managed

Tell that to the marines! The US Marine Corps sums up its code of ethics in three words: honour, courage, commitment. In business, comparable codes exist. They form the basis for managing what admittedly is an area of complexity and diverse dilemmas. While codes of behaviour do not guarantee an ethical culture, they do clarify desired behaviour and articulate for employees what is expected of them.

Perhaps some of your colleagues remain sceptical, believing that 'we can't manage values'? Just be willing to remind them gently that management itself is a value system.

GSK

GSK, the pharmaceutical company, manages values through diverse means. These include the leadership requirement for everyone in the company to 'demonstrate the highest integrity in their conduct by actions such as: not offering illegal inducements to anyone; safeguarding company assets; making realistic commitments and meeting them; doing the right thing for GSK, not just ourselves or the team; looking for principles not loopholes; seeking guidance when in doubt.'[7]

Myth no 6: We've never broken the law so we must be ethical

Many perfectly legal actions can still be deeply unethical. You can probably think of many. Some common examples are: a company becomes aware that its products are faulty and even life threatening. Yet it deliberately delays recall, while still meeting strictly legal requirements to do so. Or certain people constantly complain about colleagues, which, while not illegal, yet may cause real distress. Or advertising makes bold product claims which are strictly within the law, yet nevertheless misleads.

If you encounter this myth in your organization, begin posing some simple questions and it's likely to dissipate, like early morning mist. For example: Shouldn't we be concerned with someone withholding information about a product failure? Do we not care if a manager massages a department budget or sales figures into making them look more favourable? Can we really accept a persistent breach of customer confidentiality?

Like putting a frog in cold water, and heating it up gradually so that the frog doesn't notice until too late, unethical behaviour often starts with something fairly low key which initially goes unnoticed. Eventually though, it can transform into something far more lethal. Finally, remind colleagues how every management decision ultimately has an ethical dimension. You just have to be aware of it.

Myth no 7: Unethical behaviour in business is just due to a few 'bad apples'

'We were all at it.' A tabloid journalist revealed the true situation about unethical practices at the *News of the World*, prior to its closure: 'It wasn't a sideline undertaken by a few bad apples, it WAS the job. We set up the deals and the execs signed-off on them.'[8]

Most unethical behaviour in business happens because the environment supports it, either by encouraging it or through benign neglect. When it comes to ethics, most people tend to be followers, and if told to do something unethical will tend to do so; they must be led towards doing the right thing.

Moving beyond the myths

Myths alone do not explain the difficulties you may face in moving the organization towards an ethical culture. There are other practical obstacles that make it clear why creating an ethical culture depends so heavily on effective and committed leadership (Figure 3.1).

By far the biggest obstacle to moving towards an ethical culture is the complexity of your organization. In particular, the existing culture will heavily influence the response to the intention to move in an ethical direction. For example, in an immature corporate culture that expects blind obedience, employees are simply told what to do and expected to do it. It will therefore take considerable change before they will be willing to raise ethical concerns about behaviour that may be putting the company at risk. In this kind of culture, fewer than one in five employees would voluntarily come forward if they saw something unethical happening.

If the culture has reached the level of maturity where employees at least follow the rules, policies and procedures established by what they believe to be a skilled management team, they are more likely to come forward about misbehaviour. In this kind of culture just over half (61 per cent[9]) of employees would report unethical misbehaviour if they saw it.

FIGURE 3.1   Obstacles to building a strong ethical culture

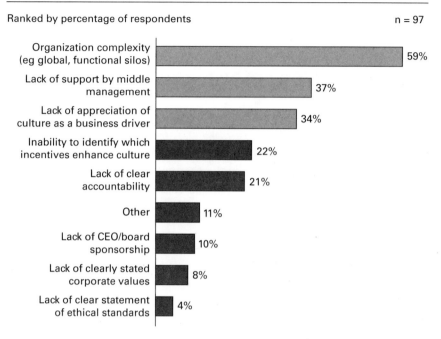

Ranked by percentage of respondents   n = 97

Organization complexity (eg global, functional silos) — 59%
Lack of support by middle management — 37%
Lack of appreciation of culture as a business driver — 34%
Inability to identify which incentives enhance culture — 22%
Lack of clear accountability — 21%
Other — 11%
Lack of CEO/board sponsorship — 10%
Lack of clearly stated corporate values — 8%
Lack of clear statement of ethical standards — 4%

SOURCE: Corporate culture is the top priority for ethics and compliance leaders, Corporate Compliance Insights LRN Study, 3 May 2011. Reproduced by permission

However, if your corporate culture is mainly values driven, people take responsibility for the culture and are inspired to align around the company's mission and purpose and to focus on its long-term legacy. If you achieve this situation, it has considerable and attractive payoffs. For example, over three out four employees (89 per cent) would come forward if they saw unethical behaviour. Better still, however you measure performance, these values-driven organizations do better than other types of organization. They produce higher levels of innovation, employee loyalty and customer satisfaction, lower levels of misconduct, and superior overall financial performance.[10]

In wondering how to produce your own intended culture shift, you might sensibly decide to look at the present culture. This can provide clues about how best to tackle the intended change. There are numerous cultural surveys that can throw fresh light on 'the way things really happen around this place'. They can help you unravel the forces driving current organizational behaviour. You gain more insight into the impact that these forces make on real outcomes and performance, including a readiness to report on ethical dilemmas. Armed with this picture of what is happening, you will be better equipped to develop your change strategy.

Building a strong ethical foundation

An important puzzle to solve is: 'How do I start putting ethics on the corporate map?' Or more simply: 'Where do I start?' And having started: 'How do I make sure that ethical behaviour becomes a normal part of the corporate culture?' This last question is about ensuring that you sustain changes, resisting the inevitable negative effects of a slow return to the previous status quo – what experts call the steady drain of entropy.

To answer these perfectly sensible questions, let's start with an analogy. No one would dream of erecting a large building like the London Shard without having a detailed architectural design. This is what guides the army of builders, quantity surveyors and construction engineers. This would be incomplete without lists of materials and a description of the essential foundations. Similarly, building an ethical culture depends on the right plan and putting the foundations in place (Figure 3.2). So let's review the essential building blocks for creating the kind of ethical culture you have in mind. These all appear in more detail below except for 'Behaviours', which are discussed in the following chapters.

Values drive ethical cultures. In describing its culture, for example, Netflix explains: 'Values are what we value.'[11] They tell us how to behave, for example, respect, honesty, fairness, responsibility. These moral values or ethical principles are the engine powering any attempt to establish a corporate social conscience – whether from the ground up, or by shifting an existing one.

In ethical cultures where people regularly refer to values to decide what is right and wrong, they are more likely to take personal responsibility for their actions. They have the confidence to draw on their own inbuilt sense of what is the ethical thing to do.

FIGURE 3.2 Foundations for a sustainable ethical culture

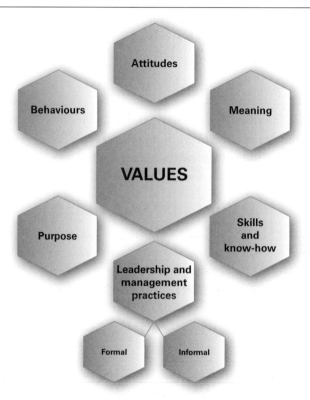

Be sure to put values at the centre of your efforts to generate an ethical culture – articulating them, gaining commitment to them, showing what they mean for daily activities, and publicizing them in action.

> The upmarket retail firm Nordstrom relies on its employees understanding its values to guide their decisions. Famously, it gives them a small handbook containing 75 words concluding with: 'Nordstrom Rules: Rule #1: Use best judgment in all situations. There will be no additional rules.'

Attitudes are often a hidden side of a corporate culture. For example, if research into employee attitudes reveals that most people do not trust management, you can be sure that this will adversely affect how they handle ethical dilemmas. In creating an ethical culture, uncover people's prevailing attitudes and assess how these may be affecting their approach to dealing with right and wrong. Do these attitudes align with the current corporate values?

For example, suppose a large proportion of your employees feel reluctant to speak up about potentially unethical practices. It's a clear sign of the need for new ways of raising confidence levels, so that people feel able to report such incidents and to confront wrongdoing.

> At the trial of USB trader Kweko Adoboli in 2012, the jury heard that colleague John Hughes had failed to report him for a second time, after discovering him breaking the daily limit in June 2011, because of how the previous episode had affected their professional relationships. Asked why he had not reported Mr Adoboli's behaviour earlier, he said: 'I wish I had done. Then we would not be here.'[12]

One of the benefits of an ethical culture is that people come to see their work as worthwhile. That is, they find meaning in what they are doing. Motivation research confirms that while financial rewards are important, pay is seldom a prime motivator. Despite this oft-confirmed fact, there continues a disconnect between what employers *think* people want from work and what they *say* they want.

It is important not to underestimate people's need to do good, make a difference and feel that their work matters. For example, what gives work meaning will be the chance to contribute, flexible work schedules, opportunities for advancement, recognition, and a sense of belonging. The decline of companies as communities in which people care for something larger than themselves helps explain the collapse of once-great corporations and ethical failures like the subprime mortgage fiasco in the United States which sparked the Great Recession. When people feel a true connection, a sense of meaning and belonging, they are more likely to actively support the aims of an ethical culture and to speak up in support of it.

Ethical corporate cultures need to be grounded on a clear purpose. People need to know 'why we're here'. Working for a pharmaceutical company, for example, which says that its main purpose is to make money for its share-holders, may have limited appeal, compared to the rather higher purpose of saving lives through the development of new health-care products.

People look to the organization's senior leaders to demonstrate a worth-while purpose. For example, they want to be inspired with the vision and raison d'être of the organization. Employees quickly detect if the purpose of their organization lies at odds with the one stated by its leaders and managers. If they don't understand or support the purpose, they are unlikely to fully support the declared aim of an ethical culture.

Ethical situations pose dilemmas: 'Should I report this; what should I do about what I have just seen; who should I tell about this behaviour; is that right or wrong; are our formal rules of conduct being followed?'

If your people are to behave ethically they must have the confidence to handle uncomfortable conversations about questionable behaviour. You may need to take special steps to ensure that they acquire new skills and understanding in dealing with such situations.

As a leader or manager, what you do every day directly affects the formation and maintenance of the corporate social conscience. For example, do you walk the talk and demonstrate integrity, or merely urge others to do what's right? The classic example is where managers stress the importance of quality in production, yet allow shoddy goods or service to prevail, despite warnings about the issue.

The formal and informal practices of leaders and managers influence ethical behaviour. Do these work closely together – are they properly aligned? For example, how consistent are the respective messages reaching employees about acceptable and unacceptable forms of behaviour?

The formal system is the role played by the management structure in reinforcing ethical values. This includes processes such as:

- How decisions are made: is an ethical filter put on all major ones?

- A proper system for hiring the right people: does it weed out potential wrongdoers, or those who will not subscribe to the corporate values?

- An appropriate management structure: is it weighted down with hierarchy or more inclusive? Long lines of accountability with many layers of responsibility, for example, can make it difficult to monitor standards and may prevent people from feeling able to tackle ethical abuses.

- A formal written ethical code and set of policies: is there one that everyone helped to devise? Do people in the organization both understand it and refer to it when necessary? (See page 57).

Beyond these, there needs to be an ethical compliance system that rigorously tackles non-compliance. For example, GSK 'has an active system of internal management controls to identify risks, issues, and incidents with appropriate action taken. Management and compliance policy provides the framework for these internal controls.' People must see that the company is serious about pursuing an ethical culture.

There must also be suitable authority structures for reporting problems and following through with remedial action. Building such structures is an essential part of ensuring an ethical culture. For example, there have been many incidents in financial services where existing authority structures were badly designed and simply failed to work properly. Does your firm provide clear routes for people to report questionable activity, or get help to challenge potentially unethical behaviour? Is there a vigorous system for follow-through?

Ethical codes

In pursuing an ethical culture, many organizations rely on a written code given to employees. This will normally offer guidance on what to do when facing an ethical dilemma. The main strength of an ethical culture does not rest on codes, but on leadership and the promotion of values that ultimately determine behaviours and their outcomes. (See also Chapter 7 on communication strategy.)

Informal leadership practices – ones that are mainly out of sight and taken for granted – influence the ethical climate of your organization. Set out to gain a picture of these informal practices as part of the change effort. For example, do managers devote quality time to ethical issues; how do they respond to questions from people facing an ethical dilemma; is the leadership seen as authentic – that is, do people feel that the leadership is genuinely concerned to promote ethical behaviour, or is it regarded as merely going through the motions?

People soon detect a lack of top-level commitment to an ethical culture. Unless they see visible signs of this, they are unlikely to take responsibility when they themselves encounter dilemmas involving questionable behaviour.

Where do we start building?

Until 1999, paying bribes abroad was legal in Germany. In fact, German corporations were even allowed to deduct bribes from taxable income. This changed under pressure from the United States, but Siemens found it hard to adapt to the new ethics. In 2003 a major bribery scandal emerged, resulting in the company paying nearly two billion dollars in fines, with criminal charges still pending against several ex-employees.

The Siemens CEO and board chairman were forced out and replaced with outsiders. The new CEO, Peter Löscher, believed that you should 'never miss the opportunity that comes from a good crisis' and set about changing the culture. 'It's not so much the uniqueness of your strategy that matters nowadays,' he argued, 'it's the strength of your execution.'[13]

In shifting to a more ethical culture, whatever the size and nature of your organization, excellent execution of your strategy will depend on three essential steps:

Step 1 Understand the nature of ethics.

Step 2 Develop a unique plan of action.

Step 3 Be values driven.

Step 1 consists of developing senior-level understanding about ethics (see Chapter 2). This includes whether it makes sense to invest in a formal audit of corporate ethics.

While audits are seldom cheap, they can provide 'the big picture' of the company's ethical climate and be a valuable starting point for initiating change (see box on page 59). As a senior leader you may believe that you already know what the culture is, and even what's wrong with it. Yet a formal audit can produce surprises by revealing how all the various building blocks and subsystems of the culture interact to influence people's actual behaviour. Collecting this information may involve a mix of surveys, interviews, observing meetings, analysis of company documents and so on. Since the task can be complex, it usually makes sense to consider using outside specialist help.

In smaller organizations, informal checks rather than a heavyweight audit can be a good way to throw light on the prevailing ethical climate. These checks would be achieved through open-ended interviews, and perhaps a review of the organization's myths, legends and heroes.[14]

Know where you stand – the ethical audit

Audit: Do we need to conduct a formal, ethical audit and if so, how?

Metrics: What is the relationship between ethics and other performance measures in our company?

Code: Is there a formal code of ethics and if so, how is it distributed and brought to life?

Decisions: Are ethical considerations a regular part of planning and decision making; is this a normal part of the leadership agenda?

Risk: Do we conduct regular risk assessments to determine our exposure to major damage; how much authority do we give those who report on this?

Proactive: How proactive are we in the area of ethics, culture and corporate citizenship; what do managers need from the board and senior leadership in this area; is unethical behaviour dealt with swiftly, regardless of rank; who is driving ethics and compliance in the company?

Employees: How actively are people encouraged to speak up about unethical behaviour; do employees take responsibility for encouraging, reporting on and promoting ethical behaviour; do managers regular review people's performance for ethical behaviour?

Talent: Do we ensure a sound relationship between sound ethics and retaining great talent; are ethics built into the selection process?

Leadership: What tone does the leadership set for ethics, integrity and transparency; is there consistency of message between the board, the CEO and other seniors?

Training: Apart from explaining codes and rules, do we offer everyone ethics training; are managers trained in ethical decision making and how effective is this?

Blocks: What are the blocks to ethical conversations and the implementation of ethical practices and procedures; how can we overcome these?

In Step 2 you create a unique plan of action for developing your organization's moral conscience and adopting a more ethical culture. This requires strategy, not an instant tactic. It involves quality planning time to work through the implications. For example, you will need to explore how best to obtain buy-in for the change, and also how you will ensure that the foundations of corporate ethical culture such as values, attitudes, purpose, skills and so on will combine to reinforce the change.

It can be tempting to make instant management pronouncements about ethics, to issue corporate propaganda about the importance of ethical actions and circulate elaborate written behaviour codes. These treat ethics as an exercise in branding, where most of the effort goes on communication and clever ways to get the basic message across to people. In isolation from a strategic plan, though, such actions will make little difference.

Nor will installing off-the-shelf prescriptions. Superficially, these packaged solutions can look attractive in terms of speed and cost. Yet they have serious limitations, such as 'spray and pray'. This is when specialist consultants selling them 'spray' the organization with values along with lengthy procedures, and just hope that these will make a difference. It ends up being an expensive way of failing to achieve a culture shift.

Step 3 makes sure that the pursuit of change is driven by values. It's important to obtain early agreement among senior leaders on what are the core values driving the organization, and whether these have an ethical component. Done well, this can give your change effort considerable momentum. The plan for change needs senior management to state their moral principles with sufficient clarity to provide a clear guideline for all the activity that may follow. For example, DHL, the logistics company, found that having stated its moral principles, it ended up with too many corporate values to be practical. Consequently, it distilled these down into just two: Results and Respect. It is hoped that these will provide a sufficient guide for all future efforts around affecting the ethical culture (see Figure 3.3).

One of the essential tests for a corporate value is: Do people understand it? And can they relate it to their own personal values? For example, Netflix rejects elaborate rules about expenses, entertainment, gifts and travel. Instead it relies on just five words: 'Act in Netflix's Best Interest.' Corporate ethical values must make demands on people, beyond just requiring them to be law abiding. For example, in asking for people to adopt the value of respect, no number of formal rules will cover all eventualities. This is why 'doing what's morally right' places an obligation on all employees to find their own route through the moral maze, albeit helped by training, guidance, leaders modelling the way, codes and so on.

FIGURE 3.3 DHL's new leadership framework

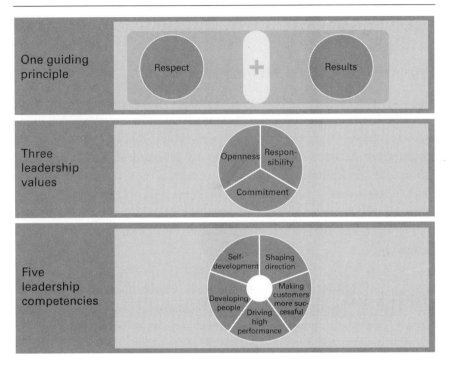

One guiding principle	Respect + Results
Three leadership values	Openness / Respon-sibility / Commitment
Five leadership competencies	Self-development / Shaping direction / Making customers more successful / Driving high performance / Developing people

SOURCE: DHL, reproduced by permission

A systems approach

'Corporate culture is crucial to creating and maintaining an ethical environment, but culture is notoriously difficult to shape and change. Doing so requires a systems framework approach.'

SOURCE: The Ethical Enterprise: Doing the right things in the right ways, today and tomorrow, American Management Association, 2006

As we have seen, both culture and ethics are moving targets and can be tricky to pin down precisely. The best way forward is to adopt a simple framework, or systems approach, on which to base your plan of action. You can share this with your key people to show what's involved and what must be tackled in a proactive way. (See pages 62–63.)

This framework will differ for each organization, including your own. It should, though, highlight the main parts of the landscape – acting as a contour map of the ethical territory you must traverse. A framework we have used successfully with clients divides the territory in two distinct ways: organizational perspective and individual perspective.

Organizational perspective

The organizational perspective takes a macro view of your organization, highlighting the main touch-points for moving towards an ethical culture. It reduces the complexity normally involved to just five basic areas of activity: a Driving Force, Leadership and Management Practices, Systems, Communication, and Championing/Modelling. You can use these like a contour map for the journey and it will normally prove helpful in explaining to others the proposed journey for creating a more ethical culture. These basic activities appear in Figure 3.4 and we explore each of them further in subsequent chapters.

FIGURE 3.4 Change chart

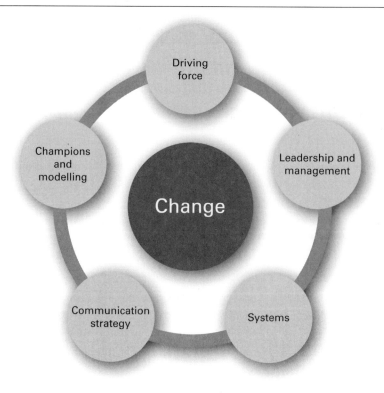

Individual perspective

The individual perspective is a micro view of an ethical culture shift. This perspective places individual behaviour at the heart of the change effort. It involves: Will, Skill, Rehearse, Support, and Rewards. Figure 3.5 shows these five key areas of the individual perspective and we explore each of them in the following chapters.

FIGURE 3.5 Individual chart

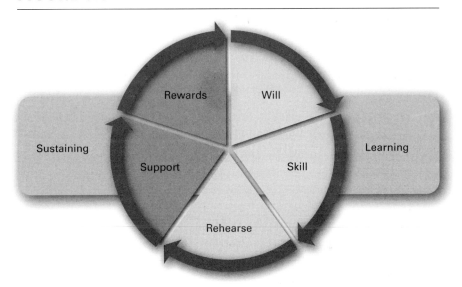

The micro view focusing on individuals raises the all-important question:

How do we make sure people actually start behaving more ethically?

Such is the emotive nature of ethics that this perspective is often forgotten or ignored during formal planning procedures. Nor are the reasons for seeking a shift towards an ethical culture always expressed plainly. Rather than saying 'We want better ethical behaviour from you', managers and leaders may prefer to approach the need more obliquely, saying they want:

● employees to be more proactive on ethical matters;
● less silo mentality;
● greater willingness to take responsibility;
● reduced fear of speaking out;

- people knowing what's right and what's wrong;
- employees acting on stated values;
- greater acceptance of diversity and its implications.

However, avoiding being straightforward and stating explicitly that you want employees to take ethical issues more seriously is a mistake. People need to hear from their leaders that ethics matter, that they are a priority and that unethical behaviour will not be tolerated.

A step-by-step approach

Because each organization must assess its own unique situation and potential for change, a universal set of steps towards an ethical transformation should be treated with caution. Certainly one unambiguous step, as already indicated, is clarifying values. Figure 3.6 shows one attempt to present cultural transformation as a personalized nine-stage process.

Entropy

Sustaining an ethical culture is a continual creative challenge. You are up against not just the natural forces of corporate inertia. There is also the well-known tendency of any system to experience the ravages of entropy, that is, a gradual tendency to disorder.

As you move towards an ethical culture, build in ways to constantly renew and review progress. In any organization there needs to be some bureaucratic systems and processes and ways to encourage decision making. But these can become mired in hierarchy and rigid silo-driven structures. In combination these can undermine the basic ethical intentions. Putting it slightly differently, you cannot rely mainly on formal systems such as codes of conduct and compliance teams to create a sustainable ethical culture.

According to the Barrett Values Centre (BVC) which helps leaders measure and manage cultures, cultural entropy happens at three levels of organizational consciousness:

- *Level 3: self-esteem consciousness* – factors that slow the organization down and prevent rapid decision making, such as hierarchy, bureaucracy and confusion.

FIGURE 3.6   Whole system change: nine-step process

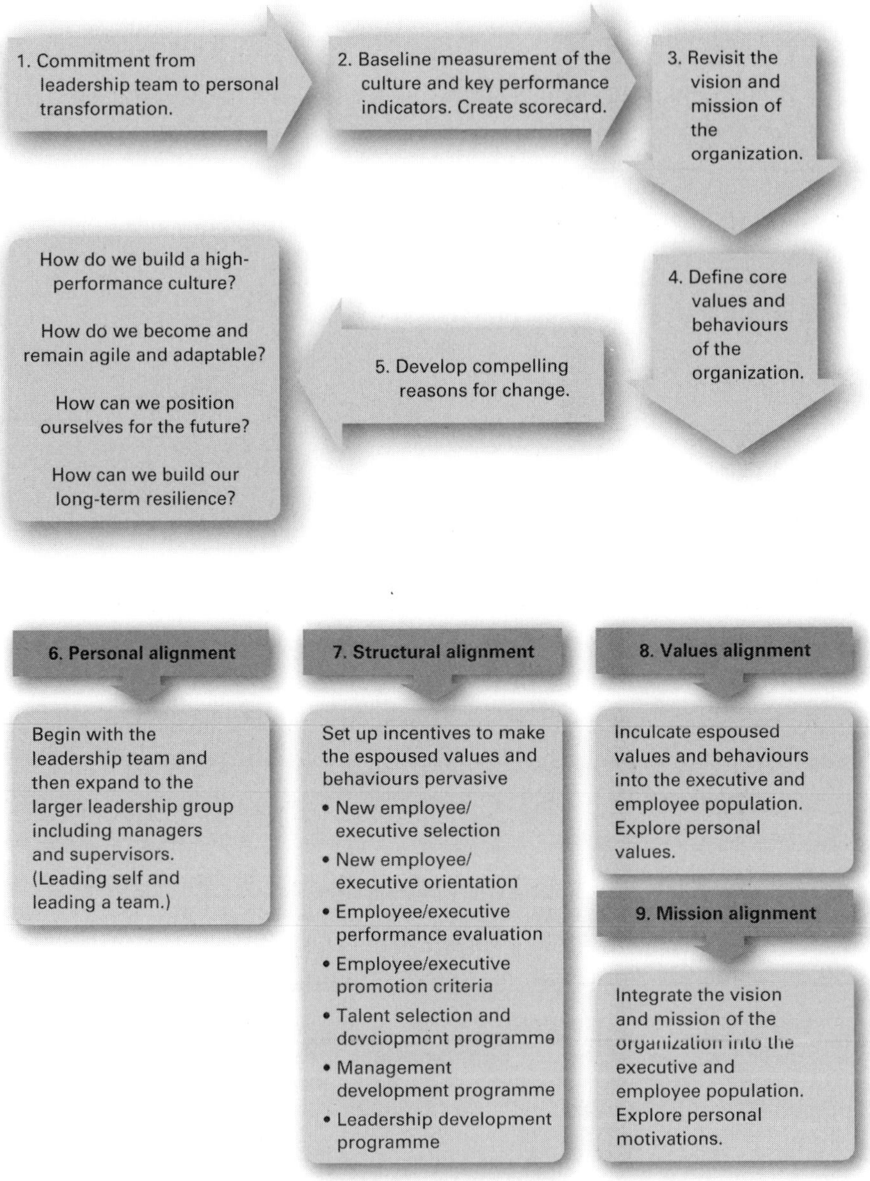

1. Commitment from leadership team to personal transformation.

2. Baseline measurement of the culture and key performance indicators. Create scorecard.

3. Revisit the vision and mission of the organization.

How do we build a high-performance culture?

How do we become and remain agile and adaptable?

How can we position ourselves for the future?

How can we build our long-term resilience?

5. Develop compelling reasons for change.

4. Define core values and behaviours of the organization.

6. Personal alignment

Begin with the leadership team and then expand to the larger leadership group including managers and supervisors. (Leading self and leading a team.)

7. Structural alignment

Set up incentives to make the espoused values and behaviours pervasive
- New employee/ executive selection
- New employee/ executive orientation
- Employee/executive performance evaluation
- Employee/executive promotion criteria
- Talent selection and development programme
- Management development programme
- Leadership development programme

8. Values alignment

Inculcate espoused values and behaviours into the executive and employee population. Explore personal values.

9. Mission alignment

Integrate the vision and mission of the organization into the executive and employee population. Explore personal motivations.

SOURCE: Barrett, R (2011) Culture leadership and change, Barrett Values Centre, May, www.valuescentre.com. Reproduced with permission

- *Level 2: relationship consciousness* – factors that cause conflict and friction between employees, such as internal competition, blame and intimidation.

- *Level 1: survival consciousness* – factors that prevent employees from doing their job and expressing their talents, such as control, fire-fighting and micromanagement.

From its work in this area of culture, BVC concludes that entropy is directly related to the extent to which managers and leaders of an organization lose their involvement, commitment and connection with sustaining the culture.

ACTION POINTERS

- Discover whether your people regard ethics as relevant to what the company does.

- Find out whether employees feel confident about dealing with ethical dilemmas.

- If some colleagues see ethics as low priority, help them understand why the issue poses daily dilemmas for people – even putting everyone's jobs at risk.

- If necessary, remind people that all management decisions have an ethical dimension.

- Become familiar with the various proven and even quantified benefits of having an ethical culture.

- Put values at the centre of your efforts to generate an ethical culture.

- Try to uncover people's current attitudes to management and how these may be affecting their approach to dealing with right and wrong.

- People need to find meaning in their work, to do good and make a difference. Make sure that this is built into the effort to change the culture.

- Assess the extent to which formal and informal management and leadership practices work together to affect people's behaviour.

- Clarify whether an ethical filter is put on all major decisions.

- Propose the creation of a written ethical code for the company if there is not one already.

- Make sure that your firm offers clear routes for people to report questionable activity and backs this up with vigorous follow-through.

Notes

1 Treviño, L and Nelson, K (2011) *Managing Business Ethics: Straight talk about how to do it right*, 5th edn, John Wiley & Sons, Inc, Hoboken, NJ

2 Currell, D and Bradley, T (2012) Greased palms, giant headaches, *Harvard Business Review*, September

3 Barclays to cut back tax unit in ethics push, *Financial Times*, 11 September 2012

4 See, for example, McNamara, C (nd) 10 myths about business ethics, in Complete Guide to Ethics: a management toolkit, http://managementhelp.org/businessethics/ethics-guide.htm

5 See, for example, Treviño, L and Brown, M (2004) Managing to be ethical: debunking five business ethics myths, *Academy of Management Executive*, 18 (2)

6 Leeson, N (1999) *Rogue Trader*, new edn, Sphere, London

7 GSK Code of Conduct: One Company, One Approach

8 *News of the World* scandal – here's what REALLY happened: a confession from a tabloid hack, WOWnews, http://wownews.co.uk/news/322-news-of-the-world-scandal-a-confession-from-a-tabloid-hack.html

9 Drawn from an average of various published studies

10 See, for example, Archetypes of governance, culture, and leadership in corporate culture is the top priority for ethics & compliance leaders, Corporate Compliance Insights LRN Study, 3 May 2011

11 http://www.slideshare.net/reed2001/culture-1798664

12 Wilcock, D (2012) Trader twice caught by colleague, *Independent*, 28 September

13 Löscher, P (2012) How I did it, *Harvard Business Review*, November

14 See, for example, Treviño, L and Nelson, K (2010) *Managing Business Ethics: Straight talk about how to do it right*, 5th edn, John Wiley & Sons, Inc, Hoboken, NJ, a selection of questions for auditing the informal system, in ch. 5, 'Ethics as organization culture'

PART TWO
Organizational requirements

Driving forces for an ethical culture

04

EXECUTIVE SUMMARY

- 'Pain avoidance' – not having a corporate scandal – is the top-rated driver of business ethics.
- The best ethical drivers stimulate desirable practices and can exert an enormous gravitational pull for change.
- Leaders and managers have little or no direct control over the external drivers, which include scandals, consumer expectations, globalization and the role of technology.
- Leadership actions on external ethical drivers deal with: impact, purpose, communication and practice.
- Seek to identify the internal drivers for change to a more ethical culture.
- Values only begin making an ethical impact when built into the organization's purpose, goals, business practices and strategies.
- Employee expectations can be a powerful driver to mobilize for change.
- Employee engagement is an important internal driver to exploit and no longer just a 'nice to have'.
- A new corporate purpose is emerging in which companies see more socially relevant and sustainable reasons for their existence.

Why bother with an ethical culture? If you're a senior leader there are plenty of other urgent demands for your attention. You must stay abreast of technology, competitors' advances, globalization, and opportunities and threats within your own industry, let alone keep an eye on mission, values, strategy, goals and the interests of numerous stakeholders. Ethics must surely be low down the pecking order?

When it comes to simple choice, in the West at least, 'protection of brand and reputation' is rated as one the top reasons for wanting an ethical culture. It will almost certainly continue being a major driver for change during the next decade. Even more revealing, when US executives ranked their most important reason for running a business in an ethical manner, they chose as their second-highest priority: 'It's the right thing to do.' This was not driven solely by pragmatism, since these leaders were acutely aware of the compelling contribution played by morality and values.[1]

Nations differ in how they see and treat business morality, and are at different stages in their approach to it.

In his best-selling *China in Ten Words*, acclaimed author Yu Hua sums up the Chinese business ethical scene as: '...we live in a frivolous society, one that doesn't set much store by matters of principle'. In recent years, 50 'new' Chinese tycoons have been arrested or fled to avoid arrest. Their crimes included: misappropriation of funds, conspiracy to rob and swindle, corporate bribery, fabrication of financial bonds, illegal diversion of public funds, irregular seizure of agricultural land, and contract fraud.

In Bolivia's third-largest city, two Western companies did a deal with the national government. In exchange for building a dam, it granted them a monopoly of the municipal water supply. The firms promptly raised water rates dramatically, forcing some of the poorest families in South America to choose literally between food and water.

In South Africa, gold mines are the front line in an increasingly violent battle over greed, inequality and economic liberation. Strikes rage above the country's vast reserves of platinum, gold and coal. No one quite knows where it will end.

Let's be clear, wealth creation is a fundamental social good, the question is how is this wealth created and can it be created in a more responsible way?

(Trust: the behavioural challenge, PwC, October 2010)

For many Western companies, success in the 21st century is already making ethics an almost inescapable top management concern. If you work in one of the more fractured industries, such as financial services, the media or in public bodies where serious unethical practices have surfaced, for example the police or the health service, or residential care for the elderly, you already experience the substantial pressure for change.

However, if marching to a different ethical tune was easy, most organizations, including yours, would be doing so by now. So what will make a shift in the culture possible? Taking the organizational perspective – a macro view – you need to first identify and then exploit a strong driving force. This must become a clear purpose, an irresistible reason why your company needs to give ethics sustained attention, and you must not allow it to be relegated as a luxury or an option.

> Ethical driver: a substantial internal or external force prompting a shift towards more ethical or moral conduct within an enterprise.

Change management experts know that making anything new happen usually requires a driver that generates a heightened sense of urgency. Sometimes called 'burning platforms', these hard-to-resist forces might include a survival-threatening financial crisis, a mega-dip in sales, a devastating reputational threat, a hostile takeover bid or other such dramas. Destabilizing and usually unwelcome, they have the power to upset the current equilibrium. Their presence can persuade even the most reluctant organization to embark on transformational change. The best ethical drivers similarly stimulate companies to adopt more ethical practices, to start demonstrating a moral conscience.

Like a black hole in space, effective ethical drivers may have little effect when merely described. Up close, though, when they begin affecting profits, customer perceptions, employee loyalty and even accident rates, they exercise an enormous gravitational pull. They draw the organization inexorably towards a culture shift – or perhaps, as happened with the *News of the World* and Arthur Andersen, towards extinction.

Arthur Andersen, one of the world's most successful technology consulting firms, had by most standards a highly ethical culture. It also had the best people, the best business systems, and a holistic commitment to performance ethics.

In a few short months of 2002 it went from being one of the leading professional services organizations to a mere Wikipedia entry. Its precipitous fall stemmed from a slow, almost imperceptible, cultural erosion begun decades before the Enron debacle.

External drivers

Various external drivers, many growing in strength, are pushing companies to brush up their business ethics. For example, pain avoidance is the top driver with organizations anxious to avoid malfeasance scandals, the threat of public disfavour and even potential jail time.

Business pressures are another inexorable outside force, with competitors seeing high ethical standards as a possible market advantage. Demands from customers and investors, too, are playing their part in creating the outside drive to change. Globalization and legislation are also having their own effect in pushing for a more ethical culture.

As a leader, you have almost no direct control over these 'externalities'; your main task is ensuring a proper impact analysis, along with identifying an appropriate internal response.

External drivers for a more ethical culture

- Scandals and government responses
- Legal: laws and regulations
- Business pressures – market competition
- The changing role of leaders
- Societal attitudes
- Consumer expectations
- Demand by investors
- Globalization
- The corporate social responsibility movement
- The role of technology

Many of these external drivers will already be familiar to you. Their impact, though, may be underrated or insufficiently analysed. For example, as technologies grow ever more powerful, increasingly difficult ethical questions will arise, such as infringing the rights of individuals, reduction in privacy, and the retention of private and confidential information such as medical records sitting on shared databases. Some companies already self-censor and apply internal policies to limit potential damage. The ethical question that may need to be asked is: 'We have the technology to do this but is it ethical to actually use it in this way?' People's attitudes and expectations of business are also undergoing fundamental shifts, partly due to the declining trust seen in recent years (see Chapter 5 on leadership and management of ethical cultures).

The ever-expanding army of external drivers seems an unstoppable force for change. For example, a major US study concluded that while business scandals had a major impact on business ethics in recent years, 'in the future, globalization and competition will be the top business driver of ethics'. It also predicted that laws and regulations will remain highly influential.[2] Looking further ahead, environmental issues are likely to play a bigger part in prompting ethical changes within your organization, as Table 4.1 suggests.

While external drivers are mainly outside your control, you can still take at least three major actions, such as:

- Analysis: continually assess the nature of the external drivers and analyse their likely short- and long-term effects.

- Communication: make all your people aware of these drivers and their likely consequences – at a personal level, not just the corporate one.

- Practice: where appropriate, create new practices, procedures and systems.

Analysis

People in an organization may become blind to the risks from certain behaviours and actions, because these have become ingrained in the 'way we do things round here'. For example, Railtrack's board failed to recognize that the Hatfield rail crash in 2000 could so seriously damage its reputation that the government would withdraw its licence to operate.

And some important risks lie hidden beneath a 'glass ceiling'. They occur deep within the organization and top management remain protected from

TABLE 4.1   Future impact of external drivers

Rank	Rank now	Rank in 10 years
Laws and regulations	1	1
Economic environment	2	4
Political environment	3	9
Social values	4	6
Privacy	5	8
Level of global security	6	5
Technology	7	7
CSR movement	8	3
Environmental issues	9	2

SOURCE: American Management Association (2006) The ethical enterprise: doing the right things in the right ways, today and tomorrow. Reproduced with the permission of American Management Association International

having to confront these dangers. Rogue traders are one of the most high-profile causes in the banking sector. Another is health and safety, where weak standards stay out of sight until a full-blown crisis hits senior awareness, such as the BP Gulf disaster. What would normally be an internal matter, a failure at a well head, became a threat to the survival of the entire company. Its impact on the leadership was explosive, with the CEO out of his depth and complaining that he wanted his 'life back'.

One insightful study of these unseen risks found that an important cause of crises stemmed from inadequate leadership on ethos and culture. It reported that many of the risks it had highlighted were inherent in every organization. 'Unrecognized and unmanaged, these underlying risks pose a potentially lethal threat to the future of even the largest and most successful businesses.'[3]

Communication

Consider sharing widely with your people how the important drivers are pushing your company to shift its ethical stance. Everyone in the organization needs to become aware of why a different response to ethical issues may be needed, particularly by the leadership, and if necessary, how they too can play their part.

It is not enough merely to list the drivers and say that these are a concern. People need to understand what is at stake, what failure to respond means and how they can play their part in helping the company handle the implications.

Practice

Ultimately it's the responsibility of you and your senior colleagues to translate these external drivers into a convincing and practical resource for change. Words may be helpful, but only as part of a concerted effort to alter existing practices. You may need to introduce new or altered ways of working, new systems and procedures that change how people behave in the light of the ethical challenge.

Expect resistance

Impressive though external drivers may initially appear, they may not be strong enough to trigger the necessary internal shifts. For example, see the box 'Change, what change?'. Also, some people see an inherent contradiction between the energy and drive released by capitalism, and a company having a moral driver.[4]

Change, what change?

In 2008 many people were appalled at just how ruthless and unethical some Wall Street banks were when it came to their clients' money. The reputation of investment bank Goldman Sachs took a beating from the 2008 crash, becoming a byword for Wall Street excess, putting profit before its customers' needs.

Despite this dire record, it lost hardly any customers, settling with the regulators the charges of securities fraud. According to a London-based director who oversaw equity derivatives for 12 years and resigned from Goldman Sachs in 2012, not much has changed. In an Opinion Piece published by the *New York Times* and widely commented on, he told how he joined Goldman straight from college, drawn to the firm's culture, which then revolved around teamwork, integrity and always doing the right thing for the client.

That was then. Now, as he scathingly wrote, he felt that the firm's culture had been lost and the decline in the firm's moral fibre could well bring down one of the world's largest banks. What once was a place that always did right by clients was, he claimed, now a place where profits were placed above people.

(See, for instance, Holbrook, E (2012) Can Wall Street change? *Risk Management*, 14 March)

Looking more broadly across the banking sector, the driving forces for change appear considerable. A leading UK banker promised in September 2012 'to re-define what we are here to do, and the way in which we conduct ourselves'. Meanwhile, the joint CEO of Deutsche Bank conceded that 'tremendous mistakes have been made'. In the case of banking, the noble promises to reform seem unlikely to last beyond the mandatory sackcloth and ashes stage – due to how the industry is set up and the numerous incentives to continue misbehaving. As the *Financial Times*'s John Gapper concluded: 'This generation of bankers is no doubt genuine in wanting to redeem past sins... despite that, the smart money is against them.'[5]

There are indeed plenty of countervailing forces working against a shift to a more ethical culture, and not just in the banking sector. These forces are internal and external. External forces include the need to ensure the financial success of the company, increasing shareholder value, innovations, upholding brand and reputation, expanding globally and meeting quarterly earnings. In exporting industries, the struggle to win orders may undermine all the good intentions to avoid greasing a few palms. In the caring professions such as hospitals or homes for the elderly, financial pressures to limit overheads and staffing levels may undermine the sensitive caring expected from staff.

Ethics on the line

The restaurant talk is about an obscure zoning issue. It needs resolving before the company's big project can move forward. The local official smiles over his free meal, hinting that a financial sweetener in his direction will take care of it. The payment will be illegal, but the company will gain millions by opening the facility sooner, and the local manager will gain a huge bonus.

It seems an obvious ethical no-no. It's not. Executives in the Mexico subsidiary of Wal-Mart reported in 2005 that local managers paid more than $24m in bribes to officials in 'virtually every corner of the country'.[6]

Internal drivers

If external ethical drivers have limited impact, what about the internal ones? The strain arising from trying to meet unrealistic business deadlines continues to be the most likely reason that people compromise on ethical standards. Here the prospects for change are rather better. When those within recognize how seriously damaging some unethical behaviours are, positive action may start to ~~happen. Proa~~ctive leadership consists of identifying, acknowledging and exploiting these internal drivers for change, which may include:

- leaders or managers keen to install a new set of values;
- past or potential reputational damage, arising from unethical behaviour;
- work pressures, causing poor and costly employee ethical choices;
- employee expectations, sometimes surfacing through strikes or violence;
- a new long-term internal commitment to sustainability;
- a mutual desire to stay on the right side of the law or regulations;
- wholehearted employee engagement leading to higher levels of responsibility.

Values driven

'Tell me what matters in creating an ethical shift!' This cry from the heart is totally understandable from anyone trying to make a dent in their organization's culture.

If there is a single internal driver most likely to promote the shift towards an ethical culture, it's adopting a clear set of values and long-standing principles. These help create the company's moral conscience. All strong ethical cultures rest on the basic foundation of values – such as trust, transparency, openness, respect, diversity, care.

The reason a company adopts values as its critical internal driver for change may stem from various sources. One of the commonest is the arrival of one or more key executives, particularly a new CEO. For example, Paul O'Neill, former CEO of Alcoa, made the personal decision, early in his new role, to pursue a zero-tolerance policy towards workplace accidents and serious injuries within his firm. Over time, his unequivocal commitment to this aim drove a basic cultural shift at Alcoa, as well as very substantial improvements in workplace safety. At Barclays in the UK, two weeks into his role as CEO Antony Jenkins told the bank's 140,000 staff that he would 'define and embed a refreshed set of values and behaviours'. In a mass memo to everyone, he elaborated: 'How we do business, our impact as a company and adherence to our values will be considered as important as financial targets when assessing performance.'[7]

Why are values so vitally important to the ethical shift? First, because they define what the change is really about. However, they only become effective when built into the formal side of your organization – its purpose, goals, business processes and strategies. For values to gain traction, all employees need to somehow reflect them through their daily actions. New hires, for example, must recognize these as conditions of employment.

Second, as a leader, the more explicit you become about values and support them with your own behaviour, the greater the chance of nudging the current culture in the desired ethical direction.

Third, in studies of why employees leave a company for ethical reasons, nearly three out of four say they did not think the company was living up to its promises on corporate values.[8]

Employee expectations

The vast majority of company employees say it is 'critical' or 'important' that the firm they work for is ethical.[9] This internal ethical driver may not be entirely obvious to leaders and managers until they start digging into whether and how to change the culture. For example, ethics turn out to be so important that most US employees (82 per cent) would prefer to earn less and work for a company with ethical business practices than receive higher pay at a company with questionable ethics (Figure 4.1).

Many employees, around a quarter, report seeing unethical and even illegal behaviour while at work. This includes a colleague acting in a harassing or discriminatory manner and receiving unethical e-mails on the job. When they do encounter unethical behaviour it clearly has an upsetting effect. Such a response is likely to undermine, rather than support, ethical standards throughout the company. More than one in three employees have left a job over ethical issues.

FIGURE 4.1   How important is it for you to work for a company that you believe is ethical?

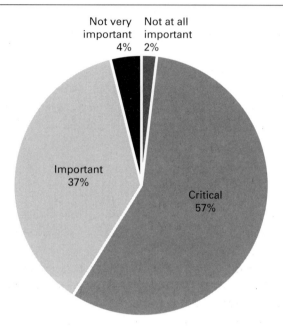

SOURCE: Employee engagement: a report on how ethics affects corporate ability to attract, recruit and retain employees, 2007, LRN Ethics Study. Reproduced with permission

Given the importance to employees of ethics, this could be a useful pointer towards conducting an ethical audit to bring into focus this potential driver for change.

Svenska Handelsbanken, one of the top 25 banks in Europe, not only survived the Swedish banking crisis in the 1990s without asking for support, but remained stable during the next crisis. Handelsbanken did not have to raise capital or ask for government support, and its shares have been the best-performing European bank stock by a wide margin. The bank has traditionally been run by management practices diametrically opposed to so-called 'best practice' in the industry.

'The staff are no geniuses perhaps, but talented and moderately ambitious people who are motivated to do what is right because it is right, not because it earns them a financial reward.'

SOURCE: Kroner, N (2009) *Blueprint for Better Banking*, Harriman House, Hampshire

Wholehearted engagement

Considerable attention now goes on achieving employee engagement within companies because of its impressive ability to affect competitiveness and performance.[10]

Engagement is no longer just a 'nice to have'. In today's increasingly competitive business environment, it's proving to be an absolute essential. Equally important, it is a real driver for underpinning ethical cultures. Only when high levels of engagement exist will employees be likely to take responsibility for supporting ethical practices.

Tom Monahan, CEO of the Corporate Executive Board, claims to have extensively researched employee perceptions and behaviour and rigorously tied them to key drivers of corporate productivity.

'What we found is a strong link between ethical cultures and employee engagement. If an employee works for a company they consider having a strong ethical culture they work harder, stay longer, and are less likely to leave. Collectively, this data points to a 9% productivity boost from ethical leadership in the management ranks.'

SOURCE: Monahan, T (2009) *The role of business ethics in employee engagement*, Ethisphere, 4 November, http://ethisphere.com/the-role-of-business-ethics-in-employee-engagement/

While engagement has claimed its place in the corporate sun, there is less clarity about how exactly to generate high levels of engagement that directly affect ethical performance. From Maynard Leigh's prolonged involvement with this aspect of people development, we conclude that it helps to view the issue as primarily one of engaging talent. Employee disengagement tends to be greatest amongst those with the highest potential within an organization. These employees are three times as likely to leave as a normal employee, should the economy improve. Yet these people are more likely to stay and become fully engaged with ethical issues if they feel valued, involved, developed and inspired (VIDI – see Figure 4.2).

With sufficient focus, each of these can be affected by positive leadership actions. See also the next chapter (starting on page 96) for more on this issue.

FIGURE 4.2   VIDI

SOURCE: Maynard Leigh Associates

Corporate ethics and compliance officers

Some companies have appointed corporate ethics and compliance officers (CECO) whose job is to look after the ethical aspects of the culture. If given sufficient authority, these managers can help move the corporate community at large towards a stronger commitment to ethics and compliance. However, often their appointment is mere tokenism and, in practice, many have extremely limited influence.

A new driver

Finally, like a prisoner newly released from a dark dungeon, a new corporate purpose is emerging blinking into the light of day. It's happening in many industries right around the globe. This is a move away from shareholder value being the almost exclusive force behind the company's actions. Instead, many companies are seeking more socially relevant and sustainable reasons for their existence.

Different industries have different reactions to adopting or being guided by a moral purpose. Some, like mining, logging and banking, have particular challenges to overcome, finding it hard to live up to an ethical corporate purpose that withstands scrutiny. The pharmaceutical industry, too, seems to struggle with deciding what is an ethical practice. For example, in France, the director of the prestigious Necker Institute claimed it was 'the most lucrative, the most cynical and the least ethical of all industries'.[11]

While this new driver has yet to reach its full potential for bringing about shifts in corporate cultures, it is now firmly on the agenda of many forward-looking organizations.

ACTION POINTERS

- Identify and exploit a strong driving force for shifting the culture.

- Consider carefully which drivers may be underrated or whose full impact may be partly hidden from view, such as globalization or technological advance.

- Positive action over external drivers will revolve around impact, communication and practice.

- Don't overestimate the power of the external drivers for change to an ethical culture.

- Adopt a clear set of values as the single most important driver for promoting a shift towards an ethical culture.

- Build ethical values into the formal side of your organization – purpose, goals, business processes and so on.

- Get comfortable at being explicit about values and bring them alive through your actions.

- Explore ways your people will feel more valued, involved, developed and inspired – high levels of engagement encourage readiness to act over potentially damaging unethical behaviour.

Notes

1 The ethical enterprise: doing the right things in the right ways, today and tomorrow, American Management Association, 2006

2 See Note 1 above

3 Cass Business School on behalf of Airmic (2011) Roads to ruin: a study of major risk events: their origins, impact and implications

4 See, for example, Johnson, P (1990) The capitalism & morality debate, March, First Things, http://www.firstthings.com/article/2007/08/003-the-capitalism--morality-debate--1

5 Gapper, J (2012) The financial incentive to behave badly will endure, *Financial Times*, 13 September

6 Currell, D and Bradley, T (2012) Greased palms, giant headaches, *Harvard Business Review*, September

7 Treanor, J (2012) Barclays 'will be about values, not just value', *Guardian*, 14 September

8 LRN Ethics Study (2007) Employee engagement: a report on how ethics affects corporate ability to attract, recruit and retain employees, http://www.ethics.org/files/u5/LRNEmployeeEngagement.pdf

9 See, for example, Note 8 above

10 MacLeod, D and Clarke, N (2009) Engaging for success: enhancing performance through employee engagement, Department for Business, Innovation and Skills (BIS), London

11 Willsher, K (2012) Doctors say 50% of French prescriptions are useless, *Guardian*, 15 September

05 Leadership and management of ethical cultures

EXECUTIVE SUMMARY

- Ethics can power your leadership purpose.
- All decisions should pass through an ethical filter which takes time to establish.
- Trust plays a crucial role in producing ethical change.
- People must feel safe if they are to support ethical change.
- People expect their senior leaders to be authentic in supporting ethical behaviour.
- It is important for leaders to set the right tone about ethics that resonates throughout the company.
- The more people feel engaged at work the more likely it is they will actively support the ethical culture.
- Raising levels of general engagement depends on people who feel valued, involved, developed and inspired – VIDI for short.

A n ethical foundation for your company is no luxury. It will power your leadership purpose and help forge the strategic vision. It can support you in persuading the workforce to perform at its best. It will also generate loyalty among stakeholders and increase shareholder value. Better still, companies where the leaders possess a strong moral compass and which have an adaptive corporate culture do better financially than those without them.

Any sustained cultural transformation must be steered by the senior leadership. However, employees see 'senior' leadership as wider than just the top echelon of management. For them, the most important leaders are local, those where they work – not the men and women in the corporate executive suite. So, all levels of management and leadership need to develop their moral compass and become permanently involved. A leader's moral compass includes these four practical tasks:[1]

- Demonstrate that ethical behaviour is a priority.
- Communicate your clear expectations for ethical performance.
- Practise ethical decision making.
- Actively support the company's ethics programme.

Together, these nurture the emergence of an ethical environment. Is all the effort worth it? Well, around the world, leaders find themselves increasingly judged not solely by financial returns, but by whether they can create an organization that values ethics and is economically, ethically and socially sustainable.[2]

Demonstrate a priority for ethical behaviour: be willing to talk about ethics in a positive way. Offer no apologies and avoid references to it between other important messages where it can get lost. In pursuing an ethical agenda, people need to hear from you and senior colleagues about why this matters to you personally, not just to the intangible 'company'.

The follow-on action is: keep to your word. Explain what you intend to do about promoting an ethical culture and deliver on those promises. Do what you say you'll do. And if you talk about ethics, others will also want their say. Encourage discussion of ethical concerns. Show that you consider it's acceptable to raise issues and thank people profusely when they do. Assure them it's alright to seek more information and further clarity. It's better to be inundated with questions or challenges than to suffer a resounding silence.

Communicate clear expectations for ethical practice: see Chapter 7.

Practise ethical decision making: within your area of responsibility, steer all future decisions through an ethical filter. While you cannot overnight change your decision making or other people's, you can require regular and systematic checks for any moral concerns. This is more than just 'keeping an eye on things'. It relies on proper systems for ensuring a systematic approach to addressing these issues and for people to regularly ask: 'Are we sure this is ethical?' (See also Chapter 6.)

Employees want to know the reasons for important decisions, especially those involving ethics. Explain these by putting them in their proper context and spell out how consideration of ethics is part of the process. In particular, start building ethics into goals, business processes and strategies. This will take time to achieve. It more important to get the approach under way than expect instant results.

Support your local ethics programme: to develop its ethical compass your organization will need a permanent programme for monitoring action. Take time to become familiar personally with this programme. Help it come to life. When you enquire 'how's it going?', for example, you signal senior leadership commitment and interest.

---

10 ethical questions every leader should ask

- Metrics: How do ethics relate to other performance measures in the company?

- Training: Do we offer ethics training to all our employees?

- Talent: What is the connection between our present ethics and retaining great talent?

- Risk: Have we assessed our potential exposure to major ethical damage?

- Proactive: How can we ensure action over ethics, culture and corporate citizenships?

- Tone: What tone should the executive leadership set for ethics, integrity and transparency?

- Support: What can the board of directors and senior leadership do to buttress corporate ethics?

- Drivers: What is driving ethical compliance in the company?

- Consistency: Is there consistency between what the board, the CEO, the senior executive team and the employees say about ethics and culture?

- Roadblocks: What obstacles discourage ethical conversations, ethical practices and protocols?

Trust

Trust in leadership plays a crucial role in producing ethical change. Events such as the credit crunch, oil spills, payment for failure, and corporate scandals are putting business behaviour under the microscope. As one recent review of the scene explains, 'The widespread perception of a growing disconnection between corporate behaviour and ethical conduct has triggered a sense that global public trust has declined.'[3]

It is not just the deterioration of external trust. Trust is under siege within organizations. Numerous international studies show a fall in trust of leadership. Consequently, employees are reluctant to speak up about potentially unethical behaviour. They fear to take personal risks such as creating conflict, suffering adverse reactions from colleagues or putting their job on the line. For people to take an interest in your company's ethical behaviour they will need to feel safe: physically, financially, emotionally.

For example, what happens when they *do* take the trouble to speak up about ethical issues? The record of those who blow the whistle is not a reassuring one. Sometimes they are praised, but far more often they are in effect punished, as happened in the notorious Ford Pinto case, where asking about safety issues became virtually a sacking offence (see page 38).

Fate of the whistleblowers

In the UK's Department of Culture, Media and Sport, a whistleblower made public his concern during October 2012 that BT was inflating its charges for building Britain's rural broadband network. He was promptly sacked after sending information to councils to help them get better value for money.[4]

Sherron Watkins, Enron's Vice President of Corporate Development, was the lone voice who dared to warn Enron Chairman and CEO Ken Lay that the company was in danger of imploding 'in a wave of accounting scandals'. Taking her concerns right to the top, Ms Watkins spelt out the seriousness of Enron's situation and the inevitable dire consequences if corrective action were not taken. Yet no one at Enron ever sought to address these concerns.[5]

More recently, Michael Woodford, CEO of the Japanese giant Olympus, uncovered unauthorized payments to third parties designed to hide losses, since estimated at more than £1bn. When the board ignored his findings he alerted the business press and found himself voted out of a job in 2011. Eventually he was vindicated with the departure of three senior leaders who pleaded guilty to fraud and the entire board resigned. But he himself ended up without a job and was thrown into what he has since described as 'the lead in a John Grisham novel'.[6]

It is not all bad news on the trust front, though. Many CEOs who might once have hidden from view are taking a more hands-on approach. The result is significant increases in their ratings for openness and understanding.[7] And if you can win people's trust for an ethical culture you will be altering the balance from compliance – 'do this, do that' – to one where people do what's right because they feel responsible and part of a community. Without a sense of personal accountability people can blame their boss, the organization or someone else.[8] However, while most people (70 per cent) believe that employees need to feel responsible and accountable for their actions, only just over 40 per cent actually do feel responsible.

For ethical behaviours to become a cultural norm, people look to their leaders for signs of authenticity and suitable tone, and respond to behavioural rewards.

Authenticity

In creating a more ethical culture you need to develop an authentic voice to be inspiring and win wholehearted engagement for the change. This is not quite as challenging as it seems. You will sound authentic if you speak from the heart about ethics, sharing your passion for why core values in the company matter. If you successfully demonstrate who you are and your genuine commitment to ethical considerations, you will help improve workplace integrity (see Figure 5.1).

Authenticity includes a strong commitment to transparency. This takes many forms: information flow, how decisions are made, and the way the company handles important ethical challenges (see the box on page 91 on Johnson & Johnson's handling of the 1982 Tylenol crisis, for example). In the light of corporate scandals, corporate stakeholders in many countries increasingly want more transparent financial reporting. They expect to see actual evidence of better ethical conduct.

According to some observers, transparency calls for a new kind of leader, someone who has integrity in their bones and who leads by example. This would be someone who 'galvanizes the firm to harness it; and who has the courage to do the right thing and the vision to build corporate character to withstand the vicissitudes of a volatile new century'.[9]

Certainly today's leaders need to be clear about what transparency means for their particular organization. For example, the Pan African Bank codified its ethical policies, which apply to directors and employees across the group. Regular reviews keep them in line with international practice and

FIGURE 5.1   When leaders demonstrate a commitment to ethics, workplace integrity improves considerably

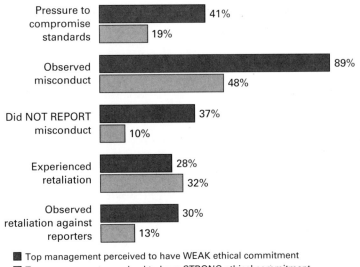

Pressure to compromise standards
- 41%
- 19%

Observed misconduct
- 89%
- 48%

Did NOT REPORT misconduct
- 37%
- 10%

Experienced retaliation
- 28%
- 32%

Observed retaliation against reporters
- 30%
- 13%

■ Top management perceived to have WEAK ethical commitment
■ Top management perceived to have STRONG ethical commitment

SOURCE: National Business Ethics Survey of Fortune 500 Employees 2012, Ethics Resource Center

© 2012, Ethics Resource Center. Used with permission of the Ethics Resource Center, 2345 Crystal Drive, Ste 201, Arlington, VA 22202, www.ethics.org

standards. The wide-ranging guidance includes: fiduciary relationships, conflicts of interest, secret profits, contracts, duty of secrecy, non-interference, insider dealing, attendance and conduct at meetings.

Johnson & Johnson's handling of the 1982 Tylenol crisis is always considered a model of transparency. Seven people died after ingesting Extra Strength Tylenol that had been deliberately contaminated with cyanide. Within a week, the company pulled 31 million bottles of tablets back from retailers, making it one of the first major recalls in US history.

This was a company acting in a manner consistent with its values. It ignored the cost, accepted the embarrassment, and certainly had no regrets over lost profits. The CEO repeatedly said that his company's Credo made it easy for him and his team to know exactly what to do: J&J's 'first responsibility is to the doctors, nurses, and patients, to the mothers and all the others who use our products and services'.

In stark contrast, nearly two decades later the chairman of a congressional committee publicly laid into the health-care giant: 'The information I've seen during the course of our investigation raises questions about the integrity of the company', he complained. 'It paints a picture of a company that is deceptive, dishonest, and has risked the health of many of our children.' A respected retail consultant to drug companies further claimed: 'At every step in this process J&J has not been transparent. Every bit of information is cagey, secretive, and micromanaged.' As one former J&J director put it simply: 'Over 10 years it became a completely different company.'[10]

It also involves being willing to bring into the open any unethical and morally unacceptable practices. For example, Project Mango at Barclays aimed to assess whether all businesses within the investment bank arm were ethically sound as well as profitable. In a presentation to investors the boss of the bank's investment arm explained that he was taking a fresh look to see if there were any products and services that 'we no longer deem it appropriate to do, regardless of financial return'.[11]

Transparency is not limited to internal matters. It may also involve proactive behaviour with external ramifications. For example, after previous ethical failures, the Royal Ahold, a major European food company, took the unprompted step of alerting the authorities that one of its US subsidiaries had overstated its revenues by many millions of dollars. It did not wait for the regulator to step in first and draw attention to the issue.

Rewards are a major influence on the nature of the ethical business environment. Employees will be far more likely to speak up about possible wrongdoings if they see leaders regularly rewarding ethical behaviour, and disallowing unethical or potentially reputation-damaging actions.

The seven transparency questions

- What do we mean by transparency?

- How important is transparency to our ethical culture?

- Would we recognize lack of transparency about ethical issues?

- What will it take to improve transparency?

- How do we reward ethical behaviour?

- How do we discourage adverse employee ethical behaviour?

- Who is accountable for maintaining standards of transparency?

Tone

'Some of the most important decisions I ever made were firing people who weren't conducting themselves with integrity', claimed Carly Fiorina, ex-CEO of Hewlett-Packard. An organization is only as ethical as its leaders. People expect them to show a high degree of personal integrity and embody the values for creating an ethical climate. For example, how you choose to talk about ethics – even whether you do so – strongly influences whether the culture develops an ethical bias.

Tone is probably the single most important aspect of being an ethical leader. Tone is set from your heart, not just your head. When we ask 'what does it mean to be an ethical leader', the answer can be encapsulated in the reply: 'It's someone who sets the tone of the organization.' It is why it requires leadership and not just management. When the chief executive of one company was explaining his new strategy, a long-standing employee asked: 'Can you tell me what it means for someone like me?' After some thought the reply came: 'Well, I guess it is all about restoring our company's pride.' Listening employees spontaneously applauded. They were responding emotionally to a leader manifestly setting the tone.

Tone is so important that some countries even try to legislate for it. In the United States, for instance, the Sarbanes–Oxley rules require companies to set a positive 'tone at the top'. A probing question you might consider for your own company is: 'Does our leadership tone resonate throughout the business?'

'The key component underlying much of what the best ethical companies do is leadership. Leadership – made visible through actions, commitment, and examples – sets the moral tone that emanates from the top of a company and that translates ethical principles into the concrete behaviour expected from all persons acting on behalf of a company.'

SOURCE: Sullivan, J (2009) *The moral compass of companies: business ethics and corporate governance as anti-corruption tools*, International Finance Corporation, Washington, DC

Although many organizations want a strong tone, they often fail to discover how this translates into actual practice. For example, when employees and managers feel under pressure and immediate business objectives loom large, do their actions demonstrate integrity? On being sentenced to a year in prison for his role in the fraud, the former director of accounting at WorldCom admitted: 'When faced with a decision that required strong moral courage, I took the easy way out.'

A leader's tone and focus has such influence on what happens in the organization that it's important to apply these to touch-points that can make the most difference. 'When I focus you know what that means. It means I expect performance', is how Philip Clark, CEO of Tesco, puts it.[12] (See also the box below on ethics and leadership touch-points.)

Ethics and leadership touch-points

- Strategy and ethics.

- Risk assessments.

- Decision making and ethics.

- Relationships between leaders and other colleagues.

- Setting ethical standards – such as how people are recruited.

- Stating norms of desired behaviour.

- Codes of practice.

- Support mechanisms for ethical behaviour.

- Actively tackling non-compliance.

- Alignment of organizational culture and strategy.

- Consistency between values, behaviours or different stakeholders' objectives.

- Levels of employee engagement.

Engagement

Nearly everywhere, astute leaders are taking a close interest in employee engagement. The reason is the cumulative evidence showing that engagement directly affects the quality of both individual and corporate performance. The stronger your ethical culture, the higher the proportion of engaged employees.[13]

Fully engaged people are more likely to support the company's culture and consequently reduce the ethics risk faced by the company. For example, they are more likely to react to misconduct by reporting what they see, protecting the company by making management aware of problems that need addressing (Figure 5.2).

FIGURE 5.2 Reporting of observed misconduct based upon engagement levels (2009)

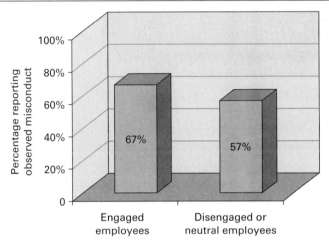

SOURCE: Ethics and Employee Engagement, Ethics Resource Center, 2009

When it comes to keeping an eye on ethics, engaged employees are worth their weight in gold. They can literally make or break the company. They can be relied on to make independent decisions and take actions consistent with the company's culture, objectives and values. They also require less supervision and direction.

It is helpful to know the current levels of engagement to reveal how much actual support exists for the current culture. There are plenty of ways to measure engagement levels. If you choose to do so, take into account both general engagement and ethical engagement. *General engagement* shows how far employees find meaning in their work and whether they feel committed and aligned to the company's purpose and core values. *Ethical engagement* is more specific. It shows the extent to which employees feel involved with, and committed to, developing and supporting the company's ethical stance.

General engagement

You have many ways at your disposal of directly affecting the level of general engagement. One useful approach is called VIDI, as mentioned earlier on page 83 – shorthand for saying that people need to feel (Figure 5.3).

FIGURE 5.3   VIDI

SOURCE: Maynard Leigh Associates

This is both a checklist and a plan of action.[14]

Being valued

One of the deepest hungers of the human heart is to be seen and understood – in simple terms, to feel worthwhile and wanted. This has particular resonance in the 21st century when so many people feel alienated and disconnected from the world around them. The need to feel valued greatly influences engagement. By comparison, financial rewards, though still important, count for rather less in people's lives.

In the struggle to establish high levels of engagement, one of your strongest weapons is how you convey the message that you value people and what they contribute. With perhaps large numbers of employees looking to you for leadership, you naturally have limited scope to get this message across personally on an individual basis, yet some of the best leaders still manage to do this using relatively simple means (see box on page 97 on showing that you value people).

Showing that you value people

- *Attention*: the common courtesy of paying attention to what people say shows interest. Even just saying 'good morning', 'how was the weekend?', 'how are you feeling today?' can have an impact.

- *Listen*: by making time to hear what colleagues, peers and employees have to say, you reinforce the message that you care. If you can't listen actively, set a time with the person to meet when you can.

- *Positive language*: find words and phrases to show people they're needed: 'Thank you'; 'You're doing a good job'; 'We couldn't have accomplished it without you'; 'Your contribution saved the customer for the company'; 'That was really useful'.

- *Document*: to increase the impact of recognition, put praise in writing. Send 'thank you' and appreciation notes and add them to personnel files; give public credit for contributions; make clear where the credit belongs.

- *Micro sessions* for those for whom you are responsible: create two-way communication sessions; make sure they are two-way, not you taking up all the airwaves.

- *Visits*: schedule visits to teams and work spaces where people come into closer contact with you – not a 'grand tour', more of a 'wondered how you're getting on'.

- *Stories*: share stories that highlight unusual contributions; give a leader's personal response to them, not just make a listing in a regular news bulletins.

- *Invite*: ask people to contact you directly with their issues and concerns – not to bypass the normal channels but in addition. Set up systems to respond quickly and positively when people show the courage to contact you direct.

Being involved

Making sure that employees feel part of the organization is now high on the agenda of many far-sighted organizations. For example, the O_2 organization in the UK retains a permanent 'Head of Employee Involvement', while retailer M&S has a long-standing Business Involvement Group (BIG). This ensures that people have opportunities to voice their views and ideas. Similarly, the John Lewis Partnership, one of the UK's most successful retailers, regards staff involvement as its secret formula for survival and growth.

> ## Enrolling support for an ethical culture
>
> - *Communicate*: 'This is what I need you to do and why it matters…'
>
> - *Ask*: 'Will you try to achieve this…?'
>
> - *Explain*: 'This will only be possible if you…'
>
> - *Describe*: 'If you do this it will result in…'
>
> - *Invite*: 'What will it take to get your full support?'
>
> - *Describe*: 'This is what's in it for you…'
>
> - *Warn*: 'Without your active help, it could mean…'

Being developed

As children we can hardly help but develop; an urge that mainly stays with us throughout life. The opportunity to be developed takes many forms and directly influences engagement levels. Everyone under your watch should have a personal development plan evolved from discussions with them. Rather than impose objectives that they must fulfil, encourage each person to arrive at their own, and then ensure that these align with your divisional or corporate goals and values.

Being inspired

Since inspiration helps drive engagement, you may need to hone your ability to affect people in an emotional, not just a cerebral way. This is where leadership authenticity, mentioned earlier, plays an important role.

Although leaders inspire engagement by what they say and what they do, many have lost the drive to uplift their people. For instance, few business professionals say they are inspired or look forward to going to work – most point to a lack of leadership.[15]

To inspire others, first inspire yourself. Recognize if you are feeling uninspired and rather than feel guilty about it, set out to renew your energy and inspiration. This might be through sharing your negative feelings with a close colleague, or perhaps nurturing your low state through outside coaching or some other stimulus.

Ethical engagement

This second type of engagement is employees showing their readiness to help maintain and develop the ethical environment. Everyone in the company can play a role in sustaining the ethical culture; you just have to uncover it. For example, you might task a group to collect stories about ethical issues, and particular decisions. Give them the remit to share the information widely.

Here is one salutary fact from research into ethics and engagement. Disengaged employees are *three times* more likely to suffer from pressure to compromise company standards than their more engaged peers.[16] The implications are clear. By regularly assessing employee engagement you can:

- identify low levels that need to be remedied;
- target specific groups of individuals to improve engagement levels;
- encourage increased accountability for reporting ethical concerns.

In an ideal world, every employee would share with you their views on how to build the ethical culture. Their collective wisdom can fundamentally guide you in the change effort. If you cannot meet everyone for one-on-one sessions, you can at least develop mechanisms that allow people to reveal what would stop them speaking up on ethical issues. For example, set up ethics committees, cross-company teams to monitor ethical performance, specialist interest groups, and micro sessions to explore and promote engagement levels and uncover blocks to high levels.

New leadership paradigm

To be an ethical leader is to be someone willing to step out and set the tone of the organization. In our rapidly changing world, what it means to be an ethical leader is constantly evolving, and the final chapter explores some of the possible longer-term implications.

Right now, being an ethical leader is already different from what it meant to be a leader in the previous century. Today's ethical leader is concerned less with self and 'I' and more with 'we'; less obsessed with self-interest and more focused on the common good; and shifting from wanting the organization to be the best in the world, to wanting it to be the best *for* the world.[17]

ACTION POINTERS

- Talk willingly about ethics in a positive way without resorting to apologies for doing so.

- Encourage discussion on ethical concerns and show that it's acceptable to raise these issues.

- Steer all decisions through an ethical filter; make it normal to ask: 'are we sure this is ethical?'

- Use the 10 ethical questions every leader should ask.

- Since trust in leadership plays such a critical role in building an ethical culture, spend time on its three key elements: authenticity, tone, and engagement.

- Regularly reward and celebrate ethical behaviour, while also disallowing unethical or reputation-damaging behaviour.

- Your leadership tone is vital for establishing the ethical culture and there are important touch-points that can make a difference.

- Seek high levels of employee engagement, since these affect whether people speak up about ethical and moral considerations.

- To affect levels of engagement, make sure that people feel valued, involved, developed and inspired – VIDI for short.

- Invite all employees to share their views on how to build the ethical culture.

Notes

1 See, for example, Ethical leadership: fostering an ethical environment & culture (2011) National Center for Ethics in Health Care

2 See, for example, O'Toole, J and Bennis, W (2009) What's needed is a culture of candor, *Harvard Business Review*, June

3 Trust: the behavioural challenge (2010) PwC Point of View

4 Garside, J (2012) Whistleblower sacked over BT broadband leak, *Guardian*, 4 October

5 Text of Sherron Watkins' Testimony at House Hearing on Enron, February 2002 (http://www.apfn.org/enron/watkins2.htm)

6 Whistleblowers (2011) *People Management*, December

7 Index of Leadership Trust (2011) Institute of Leadership and Management and *Management Today*

8 See, for example, Beyond the code of conduct: eight steps to building an ethical organizational culture, sallybibb.com

9 Ticoll, D and Tapscott, D (2003) *The Naked Corporation*, Free Press, New York

10 Kimes, M (2010) Why J&J's headache won't go away, CNN Money, 19 August

11 Treanor, J (2012) Barclays scandal forces out chairman Marcus Agius, *Guardian*, 1 July

12 Tesco chief issues US ultimatum (2012) *Financial Times*, 4 October

13 National Business Ethics Survey of Fortune 500 Employers (2012) Ethics Resource Center

14 See, for example, Talent engagement: how to unlock people's potential (2010) Maynard Leigh Associates

15 See, for example, Gallo, C (2007) The seven secrets of inspiring leaders, *Bloomberg Business Week*, 10 October

16 Ethics and employee engagement (2009) Ethics Resource Center

17 Barrett, R (2011) Culture, leadership and change, Barrett Values Centre, May

06

Systems and procedures

EXECUTIVE SUMMARY

- Systems and procedures probably account for only a quarter of the average company's culture.

- A written ethics policy has many benefits, especially if publicly endorsed by the senior team.

- It is better to design your own ethics policy to reflect your company's culture than using an off-the-shelf solution.

- Badly chosen incentives can undermine ethical behaviour and even encourage unethical practices.

- Compensation schemes help managers see ethical performance as important and realize that they will be held accountable for doing the right thing.

- Offer people simple tools for making ethical choices, such as ethical filters, decision guidelines and frameworks.

- 'Ethics' needs to run through every business process.

- Elaborate reporting structures make it harder to manage the compliance process – put more emphasis on remedial action.

Unethical decision making and wrong behaviour could cost your company a fortune. Worse, it could destroy customer loyalty, wreak irreversible reputational damage or even threaten the firm's entire existence. This litany of potential dangers has already occurred enough times for companies and their anxious shareholders to run scared. Common sense tells them that they need to make a commitment to a more ethical culture. In the unavoidable jargon of corporate speak: they need better business practices, ones that stand up to occasional and sometimes disturbingly close examination.

Better business practices, though, require a police presence – compliance systems. These are the unwelcome guest at the corporate feast. Their intimidating presence makes even the most robust chief executive wary of putting a foot wrong. Their intention is to set clear boundaries for appropriate employee behaviour from the top to the bottom of organizations and make sure they do the right thing. And they had better work. The cost of policing good behaviour was never going to be cheap and the bill keeps rising.[1]

Constructing effective systems and procedures that ensure ethical behaviour depends on diligent leadership oversight. You may be great at delegation, but you cannot simply pass on the job to administrators and hope that the result will transform the culture. Instead, as a leader, it pays to take a personal interest in the mechanisms used to promote and embed ethical behaviour and check whether they are working.

There's a fully stocked supermarket of possible approaches to select from (see the box on page 104 on formal compliance systems). They probably account for about a quarter of the average company's ethical culture.[2] With such a rich supply to choose from, it takes time to devise a manageable shopping list of procedures likely to work best for your organization. For instance, some are particularly demanding to establish, with elaborate checking procedures and intense back-office oversight of individuals' actions.

Once set up, though, complacency often pervades many systems – it's even been dubbed the 'Kumbaya' approach: an optimistic but rather naïve expectation that once a code of behaviour is published, a hotline activated, a rousing speech and memorandum from the chief executive officer delivered and an ethics officer appointed, all employees and managers will join hands in a 'Kumbaya' moment and the programme will somehow magically work as envisioned. This kind of system may look good at first. But something important is missing: leadership in love with compliance and ethical behaviour, plus a management commitment to making hard choices. Such an enfeebled system will be unlikely to prevent, detect and address real-world problems.[3]

So where should you start? Which of the many temptations on the supermarket shelves labelled 'Systems and Procedures' are worth adding to your trolley, and when you leave the checkout, which will make the most impact in producing a more ethical culture?

Policies

A good place to begin is with policies. These are usually straightforward, written statements explaining in easy-to-follow language: 'What doing the right thing means'; 'What the leadership expects in terms of day-to-day behaviour'; 'What you must absolutely not do'; 'Our core values and what they imply'. For example, Prudential Financial, Inc has a series of policies applicable to everyone connected with the company: associates, members of the board of directors, contractors and vendors. Certain policies even affect the actions of family members where conflicts of interest might arise.

In some cases, Prudential vendors and contractors must show that they understand and will comply with certain policies. They don't exactly have to sign in blood, but must confirm in writing that they will conform to what Prudential expects. The policies include its basic code of conduct: Acting Ethically; Complying with Laws and Regulations; Treating Associates Fairly; Dealing with Customers and External Parties; and Managing Risk.

Formal compliance systems

- Policies

- Rules – codes of ethics

- Metrics – measuring compliance and the culture

- Compensation and rewards

- Decisions rules and rights

- Business processes

- Reporting structures.

For a fuller list see Notes.[4]

The roll call of ethical policies you expect people to follow is useless if it merely gathers dust on a shelf at corporate headquarters. Make sure that everyone receives a copy and understands it. For example, ConocoPhilips, the energy company, requires all its employees to certify annually their personal compliance with its code, which is available in multiple languages.

Similarly, each year the health-care company Baxter does its best to ensure that its policies stay alive and relevant. It asks every executive, mid-level supervisor, sales representative and other selected employees around the world to reaffirm their commitment to the company's ethics and compliance standards. Each person duly completes a Certificate of Integrity and Compliance (COIC). This is a reporting document to measure the integration of ethical business practices throughout Baxter. In 2011, more than 14,500 employees with manager or greater-level responsibilities completed the COIC.

Putting the ethics policy in writing has many benefits, especially if publicly endorsed by the senior team. The first comes from clarifying the values and principles driving the organization's culture. Secondly, the written policy gives guidance to people on how to behave in their daily work. Thirdly, a well-articulated set of principles can be given to all other stakeholders who acquire a better grasp of what matters to the company.

Written ethical policies do more than lay down rules of behaviour. They also provide a context and a vocabulary. Referring to these, employees can feel more confident about raising ethical issues with their supervisors or directors. Taken as a whole, they form a framework within which people can decide 'what is the right ethical thing to do' and they explain why ethical standards matter.

In July 2008, BAE Systems launched a three-year programme to adopt and implement new ethical policies. This followed from a major enquiry into the company's poor ethical performance and practices. For the company to be recognized as a global leader in ethical business conduct, the enquiry proposed 23 areas for improvement.

These included: changes to the monitoring of how the company was applying policies and procedures; revised training needs and the subsequent delivery of training programmes; a programme to consult and communicate with stakeholders on the company's plans; communication and engagement with 97,500 employees.

The Co-operative Bank was the first UK high street bank to launch a customer-led ethical policy setting out where it will and will not invest customers' money. The activities that are good for the environment or community, such as recycling and fair trade.

So far, there are no international standards for ethical policies which all companies should follow. However, there is plenty of best practice policy and procedural guidance from Transparency International, the Institute of Business Ethics, and the numerous reports on ethical performance – many listed in the resources section of this book. There are also international conventions and pacts which provide useful insights.

The art of devising policy documents is one of those bureaucratic tasks beloved of large organizations. Devising an ethics policy can either be treated as a tiresome but necessary task, usually delegated to committees or HR professionals, or be a genuinely creative exercise providing an opportunity to involve a wide constituency. For example, get your clients or customers involved in the development of your ethics policies – ask them to tell you what forms of behaviour or guarantees will make them feel reassured that they are dealing with an ethical company; let your employees visit client sites to talk about your intended code of ethics in person.

For SMEs, creating adequate policies and procedures may seem a costly chore. Yet with minimal guidance and the will to tackle the issue, even a small company can achieve much. Smaller ones are often more adaptable in addressing ethical issues. Nor do they need elaborate methods to ensure compliance.

Policies are like IOUs. They describe intentions and not much more. To be worth the paper they are written on, they must be linked firmly to action. This means, for example, installing formal compliance methods such as codes and rules and not tolerating behaviours that go against these standards.

Codes and rules

From the Ten Commandments onwards, codes of ethics have struck a chord with human kind. Within a company they are the hammer that nails down policies into everyday actions that make sense to the average employee. Because people find such guidance helpful, most large businesses produce a code and around 85 per cent of the FTSE 100 firms claim to have one.[5]

Codes

Code of ethics: a document setting out principles that affect decision making. For example, the code might stipulate that the company is committed to environmental protection and green initiatives. Ethical codes are wide-ranging and non-specific. They provide a set of values or decision-making approaches that enable employees to make independent judgements about the most appropriate course of action.

Code of conduct: explains specific behaviour required or prohibited as a condition of continued employment. The code might forbid sexual harassment, racial intimidation or viewing inappropriate or unauthorized content on company computers. These are rigorous standards, normally tightly enforced by company leaders. Conduct codes leave little room for judgement. You obey or incur a penalty, and the code provides a clear set of expectations about which actions are required, acceptable or prohibited.

Whether your company needs both sorts of codes depends on the nature of your business and how intensively you intend to make the shift to an ethical culture.

Although there are plenty of templates for creating ethical codes, it's better to design one that reflects your organization's unique culture. Rather than resorting to an off-the-shelf solution, consider making the creation of your code a collaborative exercise across the entire organization. This will raise awareness of what ethics means for doing business.

Companies often rely almost exclusively on codes as their main tool for achieving ethical behaviour. But they can never be more than a guide. Many ethical choices cannot be known in advance, and codes can never be comprehensive enough to cover all possibilities. They are merely one of the many nuts and bolts of the compliance system underpinning the ethical climate.

Symantec code of ethics

The Symantec code of conduct aligns business practices and policies with company values. It provides a foundation for good governance and deals with major areas of business conduct:

- Respect in the Work Environment and in the Community
- Conducting Business in Compliance with Applicable Laws and Regulatory Requirements

- Protecting and Safeguarding Symantec's Assets
- Avoiding Conflicts of Interest
- Working with Customers, Partners, Suppliers, and Government Business
- Competitive Practices

Prudential Financial, Inc code of conduct

- I act with integrity and make decisions based on high ethical standards. I understand and honor the letter and spirit of the laws and regulations that apply to our businesses.
- I foster a fair, respectful and collaborative work environment.
- I instil and maintain trust in dealings with our customers, shareholders and partners.
- I understand that managing risk is our business and the responsibility of every Prudential associate.
- I understand that protecting information and assets is critical in meeting our obligation to our customers, our associates, our shareholders and Prudential.

© Prudential Financial. Reprinted with permission

As one major professional services firm puts it: 'While we conduct our business within the framework of applicable professional standards, laws, regulations and internal policies, we also acknowledge that these do not govern all types of behaviour.'

Metrics

Einstein was masterful with numbers. He could hold hoards of them in his head for literally months on end, until they begged for mercy and gave up their secrets. His conclusion about them therefore reflects more than a superficial appreciation of their importance: 'Not everything that counts can be measured. Not everything that can be measured counts.' When it comes to assessing the effectiveness of the ethical culture, it's important to choose credible metrics. Among companies showing best practice, the leading ones prefer 'results-based' metrics over the more mainstream 'activity-based' metrics. For example, three of the most popular metrics used are: reports on hotline volume and trends; reports on the number of cases opened during a specific time period; reports on disciplinary outcomes. Results-based metrics take companies closer to being able to understand what causes certain kinds of adverse behaviour in the first place.

Honest and conscientious employees can become vulnerable to self-deception, rationalization and disengagement if the culture keeps sending the wrong signals. Company-wide measurements of ethical performance can provide reassurance that the ethics programme is having an impact. Metrics are the building blocks of a strong ethical culture[6] and should be a normal part of any ethics programme.

Baker Hughes

An oil services company gauges its compliance programme through:

- independent audits to assess the company's compliance risks;

- quantitative and qualitative trend analysis of helpline calls by volume and subject matter;

- conducting employee baseline surveys concerning the awareness of, and compliance with, the company's compliance standards;

- matching its compliance standards to government requirements and industry-specific regulations;

- recording quantitative barometers of implementation, such as the percentage of employees trained and certified;

- comparing the company's compliance programme with industry best practices quantitative benchmarks, such as the number of compliance officers versus company size, and the compliance programme budget versus total revenue in a peer group.

© Baker Hughes. Reproduced with permission

It's important to keep the approach simple. Otherwise, the process becomes cumbersome, time-consuming and expensive. Rather than devising elaborate new systems and costly surveys, consider collecting just a few critical measurements. For example: how often are mid-level managers involved in resolving ethical dilemmas faced by employees; how aligned with the company's values are the various operating systems such as recruiting, sales, marketing, and production; how frequently do employees contact the ethical helpline?

A proper organizational assessment can help leaders understand its ethical strengths and weaknesses. There are various tools for providing a baseline for evaluating ethical practices, such as the CEBC Integrity Quick Check.

This is a five-item instrument giving a high-level snapshot of the organization's ethical landscape. It asks employers if their employees agree that:

- they can talk about ethical issues without fear of reprisal or retribution;

- their senior leaders have high ethical standards;

- the organization strives to meet the interests of many parties – not just shareholders;

- employees act in accordance with the organization's value system; and

- employees are rewarded for behaving in ways that espouse the company's values.

SOURCE: Jondle, D et al (nd) White Paper: Assessing the ethical culture, Center for Ethical Business Cultures and Kenexa High Performance Institute

If your ethics programme is devoid of credible metrics, the result will be poor management and a weak culture. And if you're not managing your culture, then your culture is surely managing you.

Decisions rules

Better, cheaper, faster, cleaner. Every day we choose, often with limited thought. Sometimes it's minor decisions, like what to buy for supper, to watch on TV, or when to brake as we zoom downhill on a bike. Occasionally, the really big choices can change our lives, such as whom to take as a partner, what job to do, or in which country to live. And then there are the important collective decisions. Nokia no longer makes paper products, car and bicycle tyres, rubber boots, televisions, personal computers, electricity machinery, robotics, and a host of other products. From the 1990s it decided to concentrate solely on telecommunications.

Similarly, people are making ethical decisions all the time in your organization. Sometimes these are strictly personal, such as whether to warn a supervisor that something is going wrong with the quality of service. Occasionally, it becomes a collective one requiring everyone's commitment, like M&S making all its stores, offices, warehouses and delivery fleets carbon neutral.

Because ethical decisions happen constantly, it's impossible to stand over people to make sure that they realize the consequences of doing, or not doing, the right thing. Nor would they consider it helpful to have elaborate directions on how to make all these choices. Not only would they feel distrusted, they would probably not bother with the interminable instructions. Yet leaders in search of an ethical culture need the assurance that it runs on clear ground rules that everyone can readily follow. So, companies often provide easy-to-use tools such as ethical filters, decision guidelines and frameworks.

Ethical filters test every decision against the company's expectation that 'you will do the ethically right thing'. Filters assume that each choice is unique, requiring people to consider the implications. (See Figures 6.1 and 6.2.)

Encourage your teams to adopt a systematic approach to decision making. This might involve discrete steps such as: define the problem, gather information, apply ethical standards and values, identify and evaluate alternative courses of action and follow through on the consequences. Not only will this encourage ethical behaviour, it will equip them to defend their decisions.

Alternatively, you could provide everyone with a simple decision framework. This might combine ethics with transparency, such as constantly applying these five check questions to choices:

- Openness: Do I mind others knowing what I have decided?

- Effect: Whom does my decision affect or hurt?

- Impact: How would I feel to be on the receiving end of this decision?

- Fairness: Would those affected consider my decision to be fair?

- Ethical: Am I doing the right thing – is it line with the company's core values?

There are more sophisticated systems such as the SAD approach, meant to encourage critical thinking about ethical choices. This involves: Situation definition – describe the facts, identify principles and values, state the ethical issue or question; Analysis – weigh up competing principles and values, consider external factors, examine the duties of various parties; Decision – make a moral decision; be able to defend that decision on moral grounds.[7]

Your ethical culture needs a decision support system, making it more, not less, likely that people will take morally responsible decisions. Leaders are there to see that the framework exists, is properly constructed, gets used throughout the organization and works well.

FIGURE 6.1 Prudential Financial, Inc: making the right choices

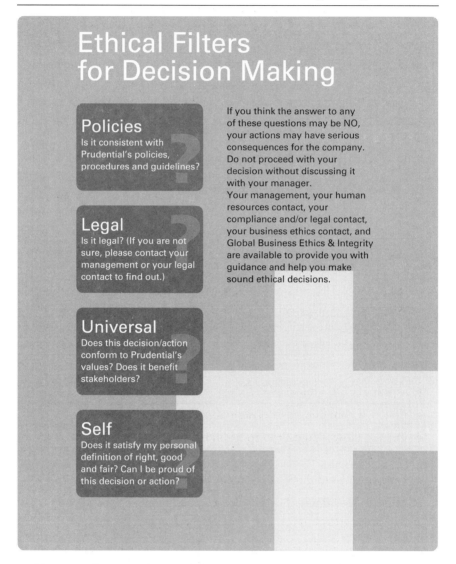

© Ethics Resource Center. Reprinted by permission of the Ethics Resource Center

Business processes

At the end of the 19th century the first words inserted into edible sticks of rock candy were 'Whoa Emma!' Like sugar rock with the lettering running through the entire length, the word 'Ethics' needs to run through every business process: decision making, communications, business initiatives, and sales. This is not being obsessional. It simply reflects continuing worldwide

FIGURE 6.2   General Mills: a champion's code of conduct

> ### The decision is right if you can answer 'yes' to these questions.
>
> - Am I being fair and truthful?
>
> - Is it legal and consistent with company policy?
>
> - Am I acting in the best interests of the company and our stakeholders?
>
> - Would I be proud to tell someone I respect about it?
>
> - Would I be comfortable seeing it reported in the news media?
>
> - Will it protect General Mills' reputation as an ethical company?

© General Mills. Reprinted by permission of General Mills

demand for companies to adopt ethical business processes. While this usually means conforming to legislation, increasingly firms must be able to demonstrate that their way of doing business is morally responsible, let alone strictly legal.

Intermountain Healthcare is an internationally recognized US non-profit system of 22 hospitals, a Medical Group with more than 185 physician clinics, and an affiliated health insurance company. Its relevant ethical business processes include:

- Respect for others' proprietary information.
- Maintain accuracy of records and reporting.
- Interact with vendors honestly.
- Compete fairly in the market.
- Use care with proprietary and confidential information that could identify either patients or members.
- Document and report events to improve processes and reduce the risk of harm.[8]

'Tell me we're being ethical.' Every leader who wants to run an ethical business needs this assurance and this means having procedures to deliver: a regular and reliable way of assessing the risk of criminal conduct; continuous checks to know that compliance programmes are working.

These have wide-ranging implications and in response to this, many companies have adopted the role of chief ethics and compliance officer (CECO). This person's main job is to help embed ethics into the culture and manage the ethical process. They can be at least as important as any of the other initiatives such as compliance hotlines, ethical codes of conduct, or formal training.[9]

Some experts fear that the CECO is mere window dressing. Having one or more ethics officers may cause complacency about the whole issue. It is rather like quality control, when a single person overseeing quality can leave everyone else believing that they don't have any responsibility for it.

The CECO's effectiveness partly depends on reporting lines such as whether this person has direct access to senior decision makers. Also, how independent is the post holder? For example, do they supervise an ethics and compliance function independent of other corporate groups, such as legal or human resources?

Having a chief ethics officer didn't help Hewlett-Packard. Chairwoman Patricia Dunn lost her job after hiring private investigators to find leakers on HP's board. The spying scandal that ensued led to her indictment and a government investigation. Even the CEO, who replaced Dunn as chair, was implicated in the scandal. And it all happened under the watch of HP's senior counsel and chief ethics officer. He resigned in September 2012.[10]

Reporting structures

'Pay is OK but the culture is terrible.' Commenting publicly about working for a certain US pharmaceutical company, a principal statistician and former employee added: 'Despite its growth, management does not have vision and inter-departmental relationship is bad due to a stupid reporting structure and lack of standard practice.'[11]

With ethical reporting, too, there is considerable potential for confusion. Basically, leaders want to know whether their ethical programmes are working. But this could mean just reporting on compliance, rather than whether people are living the corporate values. Reporting on compliance is about people working within strict rules and behaviour determined by law. In contrast, reporting on values-based programmes is on discretionary behaviour, where people make their own decisions about the choices they face. In most situations, leaders need both kinds of reports.

Ethical reporting structures are there to confirm that the company is 'walking the talk' on ethical performance. For example, the reports might:

- monitor the company's business practices;
- produce evidence of consistent ethical behaviour across the company;
- provide assurance that internal ethical controls are working;
- make the company's ethical performance visible;
- show that resources are being managed efficiently, effectively and ethically;
- report anonymously on misconduct – via helplines or access to independent monitors;
- provide access to a confidential, neutral and independent ombudsperson for off-the-record discussions about ethical issues.

Whatever the chosen structure, the form of reporting should have four prime features. It should be comprehensive, credible, transparent and promote accountability. So far, there is no obvious international standard for reporting structures. However, some companies use GRI – the Global Reporting Initiative's guidelines[12] – and the international standard ISO 26000[13] as a way of building their reporting approaches.

Danfoss – reporting structure

Danfoss is a major Danish company specializing in climate and energy services with 23,000 employees and factories in over 20 countries. The company takes ethics seriously, giving it a high priority, with a clear policy on what this means in practice. It has distributed its Ethics Handbook to all employees worldwide in 10 different languages. All people managers must sign off and participate in a mandatory ethics training programme, since they are role models for their subordinates.

Any breach of the Danfoss ethical guidelines must be reported through the ordinary management and reporting structures, or through the company's whistleblower function, the Ethics Hotline.

An external company receives and registers the reports. This ensures the highest possible degree of professionalism when dealing with cases and provides data security. After investigating a case it is presented to the Danfoss Ethics Committee for corrective actions, which may include submitting it to the Danfoss Board.

There are also spot tests to ensure compliance with the company's ethical rules. The Danfoss internal audit function performs these and sends its findings to the Board's audit committee.

© Danfoss. Reprinted with permission

Turning theory into action

Danfoss expects its leaders and employees to 'walk the talk', raising awareness from time to time. There is a simple structure for reporting ethical matters and one of the important metrics used is the number of dismissals due to unethical behaviour.

To obtain a complete and reliable picture of the situation, once a year the company asks all its 2,200 people managers if they have dismissed any of their employees for unethical behaviour. Transparency here helps raise awareness on ethics internally and is a part of trustworthy reporting, and the resulting information appears in the Danfoss Annual Report.

The company carefully compares its information on cases reported to the Danfoss Ethics Hotline with the number of dismissals submitted by the people managers to avoid double reporting. Owing to unethical behaviour there were 29 dismissals in 2009, 40 dismissals in 2010 and 26 dismissals in 2011.

Apart from mandatory training programmes on ethics for people managers, there is occasional communication on how to handle ethical matters. There is a permanent and regularly used helpline (AskUs@danfoss) to support employees and leaders with advice on ethical matters.

Recently, the company launched an ethical test for all employees in the 10 corporate languages. The aim is to stimulate interest in ethics rather than pursue compliance. The test is turned into a competition between divisions – a barometer shows which division is leading when it comes to interest in ethics. After one month there is an event with the president for the winning division.

'We know that Danfoss employees in most cases will make the right decision and will act according to Danfoss policy', says Marlene Ostergard, Director Group Sustainability. 'However, there are a lot of grey areas where doubt and dilemmas can arise. Here our new ethics test will help.'

Elaborate reporting structures make it harder to manage the compliance process. Ultimately they merely supply information; it's what leaders do with the results that matters. Choose reporting structures that are simple to understand. Often it is better to have less reporting and more focus on action.

What reporting mechanisms does your company have for supporting its ethical culture?

ACTION POINTERS

- Take a personal interest in the mechanism to promote and embed ethical behaviour and whether they are working.
- In devising systems to support the ethical culture, start with corporate policies.
- Give people a copy of agreed ethical policies and seek confirmation that they have taken them on board.
- It is better to design codes of ethical behaviour that reflect your company's culture than using an off-the-shelf template.
- In choosing metrics to measure culture and compliance, keep the approach simple; consider collecting just a few critical ones.
- Make sure that there is a clear link between behaving ethically and how the company measures personal performance.
- Choose rewards likely to support ethical behaviour and be careful that they do not in fact encourage unethical practices.
- Offer employees simple tools to improve ethical decision making, such as ethical filters, decision guidelines and frameworks.
- Encourage teams to adopt a systematic approach to decision making so that they can defend their choices.
- Provide everyone with a simple framework combining ethics with transparency using the five check questions.
- Make sure that 'ethics' run through every business process: decision making, communications, business initiatives, sales.
- Make sure that procedures to support the ethical culture will provide a regular and reliable way of assessing the risk of criminal conduct and can confirm that compliance programmes are working.
- Reporting structures should provide accountability, credibility and transparency.

Notes

1 See, for example, Egizi, C (2005) The high cost of compliance, CIO Update, 11 March

2 See, for example, World's Most Ethical Companies methodology, http://ethisphere.com/worlds-most-ethical-companies-methodology/

3 Conference Proceedings (2012) RAND Center for Corporate Ethics and Governance

4 Formal compliance systems may also include: organizational development – eg skill training programmes; recruitment and induction; performance management; detection, monitoring and auditing; enforcement and discipline; work teams and committees; IT systems

5 An Ethics Policy and Programme – What are they for? (2012) Institute of Business Ethics

6 See note 2 above

7 See, for example, Johnson, C (2011) *Meeting the Ethical Challenges of Leadership: Casting light or shadow*, 4th edn, Sage, Thousand Oaks, CA

8 See, for example, Code of Ethics, Intermountain Healthcare

9 See, for example, Perspectives of chief ethics and compliance officers on the detection and prevention of corporate misdeeds (2009) Rand Center for Corporate Ethics and Governance, Conference Proceedings

10 Clark, H (October 2012) Chief ethics officers: who needs them? Forbes.com

11 Indeed website: http://www.indeed.com/cmp/Celgene/reviews

12 See, for example, www.globalreporting.org

13 ISO 26000 provides guidance on how businesses and organizations can operate in a socially responsible way. This means acting in an ethical and transparent way that contributes to the health and welfare of society – see www.iso.org

Communication strategy

07

EXECUTIVE SUMMARY

- Leaders need to ask: 'What's the best way to communicate standards and procedures to employees and other stakeholders?' and 'How will we know people are doing the right thing and following our standards?'
- Ensure that the ethics message stays simple, focused, consistent and, most of all, 'out there'.
- There must be consistency between what different parts of the organization hear about ethics.
- Employees will only consider speaking up about ethical issues if high levels of trust exist between them and the organization.
- Company leaders need to decide: Who is responsible for making the communications strategy work?
- Apart from knowing the audience, enlivening communication depends on using the right media and effective presentation.
- Merely giving a well-illustrated ethics guide to each employee is not a strategy.
- Leaders need their communication programme to supply regular and credible feedback from a wide range of formal and informal sources.

Ever wondered how a baker creates a cake recipe from scratch and knows it'll work? Unlike chefs who often use intuition for designing a successful dish, a baker must work within clear boundaries. To produce a cake that will rise, set, and taste the way intended, experienced cake bakers would never dream of trying to bake without first 'doing the math'. They want to make sure that all the ingredients are in balance. Having the right proportions of flour, eggs, sugar and fat makes all the difference.

Communicating ethical culture is like baking a cake. You must first know what sort of cake you want – explaining codes of conduct, for instance, will differ from celebrating success at sorting a tricky ethical dilemma. And there are many ingredients from which to choose – many ways to deliver your messages. It takes planning, testing and refinement to get the ethical message across with impact. And rigorous checking on performance makes all the difference between success and failure.

Given the ethical disasters in so many corporations in recent years, leaders are right to devote precious resources to steering the communication strategy. For this, two basic questions need answers: 'What's the best way to communicate standards and procedures to employees and other stakeholders' and 'How will we know people are doing the right thing and following our standards?'

Despite impressive spending, many attempts at answering these two leadership concerns amount to mere data shuffling. For your own communications strategy programme to rise above the pedestrian, consider adopting what leaders in this field already do. This appears in summary form in Figure 7.1.

The overall goal is to achieve ethical awareness throughout the organization, which includes people knowing what to do and how to do it. Leaders in pursuit of this strategy should encourage and expect:

- a free flow of communications;
- a targeted approach;
- alignment of message;
- trust in managers and leaders;
- accountability for results;
- enlivening communication;
- persistent monitoring.

Each of these requires leadership involvement, not total hands-off delegation. The leader's role is not to do everything personally, but to direct

FIGURE 7.1   Communications strategy

sufficient attention to detail to produce a viable result. None need cost the earth. The most experienced ethical companies often find ingenious and cost-effective ways of achieving them.

A continuous free flow of communications

'We hardly ever talk about values and no, I don't think I've ever heard my manager mention ethical behaviour.' Many employees will respond along these lines, when probed about the company's ethical message. Why does this occur? What stops them and their managers from speaking about questionable behaviour happening right in front of them?

Getting managers to talk to employees about ethics is much like parents talking to their children about sex. Parents know that sex education makes sense, but find it difficult to broach the subject. Similarly, many managers are reluctant to begin conversations about ethics and even more resistant to discussing them with fellow managers. First, they worry about causing upset and disharmony. Second, some regard doing the right ethical thing as pointless, a barrier to getting the job done. And third, they fear that discussions about ethics mean losing personal power, because colleagues or their immediate boss will label them impractical or idealistic.[1]

Reluctance to speak about ethics, values or business behaviour is 'moral muteness'. It is silence despite judging some activities as harmful. Managers witness discrimination against minorities, know that colleagues are padding expense accounts, observe the misuse of executive perks or see the cavalier disregard for legitimate complaints from particular customers – and say nothing. Reticence speaks volumes about personal values and undermines the ethical culture.

It's a real test of leadership. Do you and senior colleagues have the strength of character to bring discussions out of the organizational closet? Can you through your own actions and commitment make talking about ethics issues respectable and even desirable? If you want an effective communications strategy about ethics, it involves people talking regularly with each other about real ethical issues faced at work.

You know that the communication strategy is succeeding if people in your organization keep raising, reviewing and debating ethical concerns. This is only way you can be reasonably confident that unethical behaviour will be spotted early and dealt with. Too often, though, ethical communication is a torrent of instructions, legal rulings, regulatory decrees, codes of ethics, behaviour guides and complicated compliance messages.

Communicating clearly to promote ethical behaviour

Symantec

The global computer servicing company Symantec has been named one of the World's Most Ethical Companies five years running. Ethics and integrity are the 'building blocks of Symantec's business success'.

In continuing to promote its culture of responsibility among employees, Symantec claims to have launched communication and engagement campaigns in 2011. Its publications reveal that three out of four employees with an ethics question would turn to their direct supervisor first for guidance. Consequently, the company's focus for communication is reportedly on managers – equipping them with practical tools, information and training. The aim was to help them recognize and respond well to employee concerns. Other interventions reported were:

- a new quarterly Ethics & Compliance communication to provide managers with high-level key messages, resources and training reminders;

- Ethical Moments videos and written scenarios posted on the company's intranet;
- a new internal Ethics & Compliance Communications Committee;
- better internal self-help resources;
- a 'Need to Raise a Red Flag?' mini-campaign, using the corporate intranet and posters.

Lockheed Martin

At aerospace company Lockheed Martin a series of short, easy-to-follow videos called Integrity Minute bring real-life work dilemmas to life. Topics include:

- Conflict of Interest, Outside Business Activities, and Misuse of Company Assets;
- Voicing your Values, Performance Management, and Fear of Retaliation;
- Prohibited Behaviour on Social Media, Harassment in the Workplace, Privacy, and Computer Misuse;
- Customer Relations, Honesty, Personal Security, Corruption, Retaliation, and Behaviour Outside of Work.

See, for example, **http://www.lockheedmartin.com/us/who-we-are/ethics/iminute/ archive.html**.
© Lockheed Martin. Reprinted with permission

Constructing a free flow of information about ethical issues is an art, not a science. It depends heavily on understanding your audience and choosing the right media (see below). There is a general lack of effective and transparent information sharing in most organizations around the world, and this includes ethical issues. The situation is made worse by company structures that inhibit effective coordination among departments and groups. For example, only 14 per cent of organizations effectively share information and only 15 per cent demonstrate a high degree of collaboration.[2]

An important continuing role for senior leaders is to make sure that the messages stay simple, focused, consistent and, most of all, 'out there'.

A targeted approach

Phone one of the world's most customer-centric computer suppliers and their response is predictable. 'Are you an experienced user or a computer novice?' Their time is money and they don't mess around. Expert questioning rapidly uncovers whether you need the basic helpdesk or higher-level technical support.

Similarly, ethically minded companies go to extraordinary lengths to get their message across to their various stakeholders. Like computer suppliers, they too may segment the audience. For example, internal employees may have a different perspective on ethics compared to external shareholders. Each may have their own views on such things as standards, procedures and outlook. For maximum impact, communications to each must be tailored to influence behaviour.

Different targeting may classify the audience into groups such as ethical enthusiasts, ethically committed, ethically unaware or ethically challenged. This helps prioritize communications and devise more relevant training. For example, the communication aimed at ethically committed employees will be different from the communication for the least committed ones.[3] Yet further targeting might involve taking into account cultural issues, people's individual beliefs, language issues and thinking styles.

The communication strategy is never solely about how to deliver information. It is also intensely concerned to achieve employee understanding and commitment. Trend-setting companies start by identifying their stakeholders and unravelling what each audience needs to understand and support the ethical culture.

Alignment

Ethical communications strategies usually rely on a variety of methods to win understanding and commitment. This means that there must be consistency between them. The formal side of the communication programme, for example, may involve announcements, newsletters, new employee orientation, training programmes, posters, annual and social responsibility reports, speeches and meetings. All their respective messages must be aligned so that people cannot mistake what the organization expects from them.

Informal communications are hard to control and difficult to keep consistent. Even so, leaders need to watch for any tendency for messages to diverge from those received by the formal side of the organization. If formal communications tell one story while informal communications tell another, stakeholders will become frustrated and cynical.

Is the ethical message consistent?

GSK has publically declared that it believes it is essential to its business to operate in a responsible and ethical manner. Its published code of conduct is 'not negotiable or a "nice to have" document – it is absolutely essential. Every GSK employee is required to read, understand and abide by this Code of Conduct'.

However, GlaxoSmithKline has also pleaded guilty and agreed to pay $3bn to resolve 'Fraud Allegations and Failure to Report Safety Data: Largest Health Care Fraud Settlement in US History'.

The settlement was Glaxo's fourth with the US government in the past several years but by far its costliest and most far-reaching. Despite its much-vaunted code of conduct, over a period of more than a decade, the government's latest investigation found, the company plied doctors with perks such as free spa treatments, Colorado ski trips, pheasant-hunting jaunts to Europe and Madonna concert tickets.

SOURCE: Press release from US Department of Justice, 2 July 2012

Trust in managers and leaders

In late 2012, Britain's new City Minister put the message bluntly. Britain's financial services industry must 're-build trust as a matter of urgency'.[4] Nothing too surprising there, but far beyond the confines of financial services, numerous studies around the world confirm a serious trust deficit in organizations. In fact, the bigger the organization, the worse the levels of trust.[5]

Nearly everywhere, corporate leaders are struggling to regain trust. (See the box below on the trust deficit.)

The trust deficit

In 2012, in a global survey of over 38,000 employees in 18 countries, only one in five strongly agreed that there is a high level of trust in their company. Only one in five strongly agreed that they are inspired by their company to perform their jobs to their very best ability.

There is a distinct deficit in trust, values and inspiration in the workplace, with a mere 11 per cent of organizations that foster high-trust environments where employees are encouraged to take risks, make decisions, and innovate around products, services and processes; only 6 per cent observe that they work in a company that has a strong sense of values to inform their actions over time and in uncertain, novel situations.

Only 5 per cent are inspired to perform to their highest potential whereas 95 per cent are either motivated by 'carrots and sticks' or coerced through fear.

SOURCE: The HOW Report: New metrics for a new reality: rethinking the source of resiliency, innovation, and growth (2012). With permission from LRN

Despite some rather negative findings about lack of trust, many leaders are being active about trying to tackle this issue. Some are succeeding, others are less active and some wonder if the whole effort really matters – perhaps trust is just a 'nice-to-have' rather than an essential? Those running successful ethical programmes see it differently. For them, trust between stakeholders, the organization and its leadership is an essential part of their business, never just an option.

Without trust, employees too may suffer from 'moral muteness' (see page 122). They are unlikely to speak up about unethical behaviour encountered at work, if it means confronting another employee, talking to their line manager or calling a hotline. Only with high levels of trust will employees voluntarily come forward with their ethical concerns.

There are several reliable routes to higher trust levels.

Route 1 to greater trust: Engagement

This route requires regular checks on current levels of engagement, and action to raise them. Engagement is directly linked to profitability. Therefore many companies now make considerable efforts to improve their levels and rely on four 'enablers':[6]

- visible and empowering leaders – with a strong narrative, explaining where the organization is going;

- managers who constantly engage – by focusing on people, treating them as individuals, respecting, coaching and stretching them;

- an employee voice throughout the organization – reinforcing and challenging views; employees seen as central to the solution;

- organizational integrity – everyday behaviour reflects company values.

Route 2 to greater trust: Regulation

Another way to raise levels of trust is through an effective regulatory system. With well-thought-out arrangements, it can promote correct behaviour at work. These might include ethics committees and task forces, codes, compliance weaponry such as corporate ethics and compliance officers, training, helplines, an independent ombudsperson and so on.

When employees see these sorts of formal arrangements in place they start to assume that the company is serious about pursuing ethical behaviour. Also, if the regulatory system highlights misbehaviour the company is tackling with vigour, it further builds employee trust.

Route 3 to greater trust: Leadership commitment

For this route, leaders make visible efforts to show that they care deeply about running an ethical business and expect everyone else to care about it too. Once employees realize that their senior management means business about ethical behaviour, they will start responding. They expect to see their leaders not only regularly talking about ethical issues but rewarding ethical behaviour and acting ruthlessly against unethical practices.

Trusted as a leader?

To be trusted, leaders must show:

- ability – competence at doing their job;
- empathy – a concern for others beyond their own needs and having benign motives;
- integrity – adhering to a set of principles acceptable to others, reflecting fairness and honesty;
- predictability – over time, acting with consistency.

Accountability

An aircraft carrier like the monstrous USS *Theodore Roosevelt* never sleeps. Weighing 117,200 short tons[7], there is always sound: sailors padding the decks, the ever-present noises of the ship, the wheeze of the ventilation systems and the thumping of her hydraulics leave you feeling trapped in a mechanical leviathan. Her captain seldom sleeps either, never far from the bridge as important activities continue relentlessly day and night.

Successful ethical communication programmes are a bit like carriers. Numerous operations happen simultaneously, with an equal need for clear lines of accountability. When it comes to the company's ethics programme, company leaders need to decide: 'Who is responsible for making the communication strategy work?' This includes its numerous offshoots, such as regular monitoring, reporting and follow-through action in response to information about ethical issues.

To resolve accountability, many companies appoint specialist teams led by a chief ethics and compliance officer. Once established, the role is critical to the success of the compliance system and its communication. In smaller companies a senior director may do this job, perhaps supported by one or two colleagues with a particular interest in pursuing an ethical culture.

Yet another way to create accountability is hiring an outside agency with a clear brief on how it will handle ethical referrals. This independent, external provider will have the role of ensuring that the company handles its ethical issues thoroughly. This may include significant parts of the communication process to individuals and upwards to the board.

Baxter

Baxter is a global health-care company whose Corporate Responsibility Office (CRO) consists of six senior executives with a direct reporting link to the board. The CRO has responsibility for communicating the company's ethics and compliance standards, providing guidance and overseeing training to employees and directors. It maintains multiple channels for employees to seek guidance on the right course of action, raising compliance concerns and monitoring compliance.

To promote communications the company has established an Integrity-Based Decision-Making model to help employees decide the most appropriate course of action, consistent with Baxter's code of conduct and values (see also Chapter 6) and an independently run ethics helpline.

© Baxter. Reprinted with permission

Enlivening communication

You cannot bore people into good behaviour. Too many messages with multiple intentions can quickly induce ethical overload. Countless rules and instructions soon cause disinterest in doing anything about the real issues concerning the company. Yet research confirms that employees consider ethics to be important. They will often choose to remain with an ethically minded company rather than move to a less ethical company for more pay. So how can you make the ethical message lively and attract sustained employee and stakeholder interest?

Apart from knowing the audience (see page 123), enlivening communication depends on using the right media and effective presentation. For example, in devising the content it is important to recognize when expectations need to be clarified, to give plenty of examples explaining the underlying values, and to anticipate barriers to meeting the ethical requirements. There is an ever-growing range of media available to grab people's attention about ethics. Figure 7.2 shows some of those used by trend-setting ethical companies and the rest.

FIGURE 7.2   Media used for ethics communications: WME winners vs non-winners

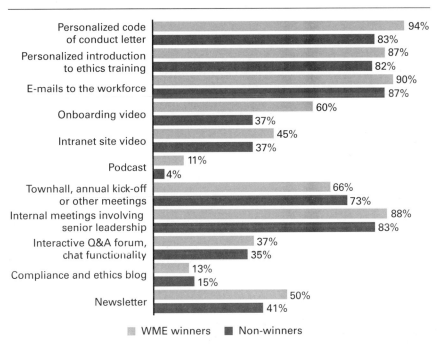

SOURCE: World's Most Ethical Companies, with permission from Ethisphere

It's important to keep measuring the effectiveness of these, since this can change over time as people become used to a particular kind and less stimulated than previously.

Leaders who tell stories are a valuable way of enlivening the ethics message. You will be an empowering leader if you enjoy storytelling and adopt a strategic narrative. This is explaining where the organization is coming from and where it is going so as to grab people's attention. Most of all, keep talking about the ethics issue regularly, and constantly refer to the company's code of behaviour.

Communicating codes

Hammurabi was the sixth king of Babylon, living nearly 2,000 years BC. He extended Babylon's control over Mesopotamia and from him we have the first written codes of law. These laws were written on a stone tablet standing over 2.4 metres tall, and were found in 1901. There are 282 such laws in the Code of Hammurabi. Moses was big on tablets too, of course, but both Hammurabi and Moses faced the same problem: how to communicate the rules to everyone else.

Not much seems to have changed in four millennia, since companies also face this issue of how to communicate their values and codes of ethics to all the relevant stakeholders. Merely giving a well-illustrated guide to each employee is not a strategy. It requires a more considered approach if you intend to affect people's awareness about ethical issues. A sound communication strategy will make sure that:

1 Every employee receives a copy of the code or has ready access to it and actually confirms that they have read it.

2 All employees understand their personal responsibility to abide by the provisions and standards set out in the code.

3 There is an unmistakeable company commitment to the code and every employee realizes this.

4 Employees are exposed to plentiful examples of the code's usefulness, and how common questions about its intent and application have been resolved.

Bringing the ethical message to life

In 'Making the Right Choices', Prudential Financial, Inc provides employees with lively examples and case studies showing what to do. For instance:

- Wrong: an associate gives her password to another associate so that she can gain access to a critical document while travelling.

- Right: an associate observes an individual acting strangely near the company garage and reports the incident immediately.

There are also many scenarios to show how one might tackle a problem. For example:

Scenario: You work in a group that relies heavily on a system that was installed several years ago. Over the last 12 months, you have become increasingly concerned about risk of loss to the company because of periodic system performance issues. What should you do?

Answer: Assess the risk and communicate it effectively to your management. Make the operations team closest to the system aware of the risk of system performance issues. Establish and continually review processes to mitigate the potential risks on a timely basis.

Scenario: As the manager responsible for hiring, you've been reviewing resumés of candidates for a role involving communications with external parties. You and key members of your team have held interviews with promising candidates, and narrowed down the individuals to the top three. The clear choice is a woman. If hired, she would be the first woman to ever hold the position. Should that factor into your decision?

Answer: No. Managers must make all hiring decisions based on an applicant's qualifications without discriminating against any individual, in this case based on the candidate's gender.

Persistent monitoring

'Show me' says the smart CEO on being told that the ethics communication and compliance programmes are working well. As a 2012 survey of compliance officers concluded: 'Few elements of corporate compliance are as elusive as the art of confirming that, yes, your ethics & compliance program is effective.'[8]

Leaders need their communication programme to supply regular and credible feedback from a wide range of formal and informal sources. But when it comes to metrics you can measure yourself to death. (See the box on page 132 on evaluating ethics and compliance programmes.)

> ### Evaluating ethics and compliance programmes
>
> - Hotline/helpline metrics
>
> - Customer and other third-party complaints
>
> - Training data (completion rates, competency tests etc)
>
> - Employee disclosures (eg conflicts of interest)
>
> - Material weaknesses and significant deficiencies
>
> - Employee questionnaires or culture surveys
>
> - Ageing and disposition of litigation and enforcement
>
> - Compliance audit results
>
> - Risk assessment results
>
> **SOURCE**: Broader perspectives: higher performance, State of Compliance 2012 Study. With permission of PWC

Most managers will look blank if you ask 'What metrics should our communication system produce that will be really useful?' This is a job for a compliance specialist. Ask for a menu of options and advice on how they could be used.[9] But the experts too can be overwhelmed by the choices.

For example, when faced with 14 different metrics, most compliance officers rated 9 of them as 'important'. Similarly, nearly all of them rated compliance audits as important. But audits mostly uncover weaknesses after the fact, rather than giving insight into current 'compliance in motion'. The solution is a mixture of metrics combined with insights drawn from across the organization, often using informal methods.

Make it an obsession

Behind every endeavour lies an obsession. It can be secret or outspoken, silent or loud, latent or unleashed. But there must be an obsession – or in organizational terms a total commitment. Only obsession can supply the emotional means to cope with the many frustrations arising along the lingering path to reach a general ethical awareness in the company. Only through full commitment can you expect to reach the quality, shape details, improve, at times innovate and keep the ethical communication process moving on. Set demanding goals for your strategy and it can inspire and challenge others to make it happen.

Finally, the essence of a successful ethics communication strategy is not the important technical bits; naturally they have to be there – the codes, compliance architecture, risk analysis and legal support. It's keeping the issue of ethical behaviour constantly alive, through constantly raising people's awareness, that matters – making ethical issues pervasive.

No communication strategy lasts for ever. You will need to revise it regularly, perhaps sooner than you expect. The ideal is to keep up the momentum with fresh communication initiatives, discard ones that no longer have the desired impact, and never stop talking about why ethics matter to you.

ACTION POINTERS

- Through personal commitment, help make talking about ethics respectable and even desirable within your organization.

- Keep the ethical messages simple, focused, consistent and tailored for each particular audience.

- Watch for any tendency for informal messages to differ from ones received by the formal side of the organization.

- Develop a strong narrative for explaining where your organization is going, what it wants to achieve and why the desire for an ethical business.

- Encourage the emergence of an employee voice throughout the organization.

- Help to force clarity about 'Who is responsible for making the communication strategy work?'

- Ensure that employees see plenty of examples of why the code of conduct is useful and how it works in practice.

- Demand regular and credible feedback on whether the communications programme is working or not.

Notes

1 Waters, J and Bird, F (1987) The moral dimension of organizational culture, *Journal of Business Ethics*, 6

2 The HOW Report: New metrics for a new reality: rethinking the source of resiliency, innovation, and growth (2012) LRN

3 See, for example, US Department of Commerce (2004) Business ethics: a manual for managing a responsible business enterprise in emerging market economies, Washington, DC

4 Clark, G (2012) Scandal hit staff must go, banks warned, *Financial Times*, 17 October

5 Where has all the trust gone? (2012) CIPD

6 See, for example, The task force engage for success, http://www.engagingforsuccess.org/Enablers.php

7 See Polmar, N (2004) *The Naval Institute: Guide to the ships and aircraft of the US fleet*, Naval Institute Press, Annapolis, MD, p 112

8 Broader perspectives: higher performance, State of Compliance (2012) Study, PwC

9 Nortz, J (2010) Measure or die! – using metrics to measure compliance performance, Corporate Compliance Insights, 4 February

Champions and exemplars

08

EXECUTIVE SUMMARY

- Champions and exemplars are a key resource for supporting the ethics programme.
- Champions may be fully engaged in implementation and others will use their status, influence and enthusiasm to persuade others that business ethics are important.
- Volunteer champions are resilient and determined but may be relatively isolated and receive only limited support.
- Champions can be particularly effective if leaders can create a critical mass within the organization.
- When champions talk about ethics it encourages others to talk openly about them too.
- Leaders may sometimes think they are championing ethics but may inadvertently be undermining them, even encouraging unethical behaviour, by using mental gymnastics.
- When exemplars take action the results can be dramatic and may even create legends with long-term cultural benefits.
- People expect to see their leaders exercise moral courage, facing up to ethical dilemmas without flinching or retreating.
- Failure to deal with unethical practices, to champion the ethical culture, is a sure way to undermine it.

'I encourage you to be a champion for integrity by engaging fellow associates in conversation and setting an example through your words and actions.' This rather stilted appeal to employees, by Wal-Mart's CEO in its code of ethics, is like many such leadership efforts – an attempt to win employee buy-in to business ethics.[1]

Most ethics programmes seek to capture the interest and commitment of all stakeholders. Yet in practice they rely for success on far fewer people, the ones committed to practical action; those who can bring to life the company's core values and its ethical principles. They're a key resource – the power of champions and the impact of exemplars.

Ethical champions are a dedicated bunch. Some will be paid by the company to support a specific aspect of ethical behaviour that matters to the company. It could be a compliance officer whose job is to publicize and police the formal written ethics code. Or an employee tasked to ensure that the company does not exploit child labour, or that it uses vendors who obtain materials from sustainable sources. The Chartered Institute of Management Accountants explains what it means for its members: 'Finance professionals must play an active role as ethical champions by challenging the assumptions upon which business decisions are made. But they must do so while upholding their valued reputation for impartiality and independence.'[2]

Other champions will be volunteers, rather than paid advocates of the ethical message. These enthusiasts are mainly self-selecting. They usually come forward because they identify strongly with the company's values. They are perhaps the most valuable recruits to the ethical cause. Leaders need to ensure that they receive regular support, especially from their own immediate manager.

Company ethical champions will also choose how to perform their important role. Some will become fully engaged in implementing the ethical programme. A few will take a more limited position by being propagandists, 'selling' the ethical message. They use their status, influence or enthusiasm to persuade others that business ethics are important.

Resilient and determined, ethical champions, especially the volunteers, may be relatively isolated and receive only limited support. Yet they play an invaluable part in building the culture, explaining what ethical behaviour is all about and why it matters. Whether paid or voluntary, ethical champions share a common desire. They are keen to talk about ethics, tap into dilemmas and affect what the organization does. Their contribution is usually positive and inspiring, and oils the wheels of the ethical programme. Without them the chances of its success will be greatly reduced. (See the box on ethics champions on page 137).

Ethics champions – promote the ethics agenda

- The CEO – Chief Ethics Champion.

- Senior leaders and managers – all have ethical responsibility, only a few will be champions.

- Employees – a self-selected champion group from across the organization, regardless of hierarchy.

- Ethics professionals – people with specialist responsibilities, eg compliance, HR, vendor standards etc.

- External stakeholders – certain shareholders, influential customers, independent agencies.

In pursuing an ethical culture, organize a systematic search to locate your champions, rather than leaving it to chance for them to somehow emerge. They may be found anywhere in the organization, at any level of the hierarchy. Once recruited, they are invaluable allies. However, some champions are more desirable than others. When HR development specialists choose to act as champions, they rarely possess sufficient leverage to promote new behaviours in a sustained way. Invariably they end up relying on line managers and frontline supervisors to integrate new behaviours into normal ways of working.

If possible, look for a critical mass of champions in the company and bring them together to explore how they can become more than the sum of the parts. For example, as a group they can develop a sense of joint pride in what they do, the feeling that they are all engaged on a worthwhile task. They can provide each other with support and encouragement for what can often be a thankless and lonely road to travel.

When champions talk about ethics it directly affects whether employees feel encouraged to talk openly about this issue. It influences their willingness to come forward voluntarily when they see behaviour they know is wrong. Yet leaders who think they are championing an ethical message may inadvertently encourage or endorse unethical behaviour through using mental gymnastics that undermine the ethical message (Table 8.1).[3]

TABLE 8.1 Mental gymnastics

Mind game	Method	Impact
Need to be liked	Overlook transgressions because you want to keep the peace, fear to upset people, desire to keep colleagues on your side	Instinctively people detect this leadership weakness; the more ruthless take advantage of it to continue unethical practices
Making positive	You compare unethical behaviour in your own company favourably with that of others: 'Yes we do this, but look what they do, it's even worse'	The implicit message is that whatever you are doing wrong is really alright and so you carry on doing it
Overconfidence	You think your abilities are greater than they actually are, so you discount other people's perceptions and overlook their insights and talents	A sure way to cut yourself off from important information and ideas and you may miss vital warnings about ethical misbehaviour; ideas to promote ethical behaviour are less likely to emerge
Quickly simplify	Economists call this 'satisficing'. You go for easy-to-formulate, familiar alternatives; good enough is good enough	Ethical dilemmas often benefit from creative thinking to explore ideas beyond the usual responses

SOURCE: adapted from Kerns, C (2003) Leaders do bad things: mental gymnastics behind unethical behaviour, *Graziardo Business Review*, **6** (4). With permission

Role models

> *Example is leadership.* ALBERT SCHWEITZER, GERMAN THEOLOGIAN, MUSICIAN, PHILOSOPHER, PHYSICIAN AND MEDICAL MISSIONARY

Equally important for pursuing the ethical agenda are the exemplars. A mass memo from Antony Jenkins, CEO of Barclays, in 2012 to all staff made clear what this meant for everyone in the bank. The bank's leadership, he explained, 'will be tasked and supported to be visible exemplars and champions of these values and behaviours'.[4]

When exemplars take action, it can be dramatic. In setting an example, their behaviour may surprise, thrill and inspire people. They may even create company legends with long-term benefits for the culture. As enthusiasts they are courageous, willing to show by their actions what 'doing the right ethical thing' means in practice. They put themselves on the line to send a strong message to their target audience.

Most senior executives are well aware of their impact and responsibilities concerning ethics. Yet how they choose to act in respect of ethics is a true test of character. Too many are fuelled by ambition, driven by greed, and lose perspective, rationalizing unethical behaviours by adopting mind games to tolerate bad behaviour, so long as it improves the bottom line. (See Table 8.1 on mental gymnastics.)

People expect to see their leaders exercise moral courage: that is, facing up to ethical dilemmas and moral wrongdoing without flinching or retreating. If leaders ignore ethics enforcement or simply talk the talk without walking the walk, then trying to establish and sustain an ethical culture is doomed. All the ethics programmes in the world won't help.[5] (See the box on page 143 on doing the right thing.)

The importance of modelling, or being an exemplar, is now well established in how organizations achieve any kind of major change. For example, when Maynard Leigh worked with a leading supermarket chain, the aim was to encourage the staff to be more customer-minded. What enabled this to happen was when many of the staff began seeing their own store manager demonstrating new ways of behaving.

In contrast, a code of practice and ethics courses may make little difference if senior managers do not model the way. Few financial institutions have done more than Citigroup to address ethical problems and attempt to instil an ethical culture. In 2003, the new CEO asked all 300,000 employees in 100 countries to adhere to a new code of conduct.

Yet despite huge efforts to embed the code through training programmes and ethics courses, Citigroup's London operations became mired in controversy that raised important ethical issues. Managers allowed suspended traders to return to work and there was no news of anyone being fired. It undermined the morale of those who did believe in the values. As one anonymous employee reportedly pointed out, 'Not to fire these bond traders or their management is to internally celebrate their doings and it has led to an uncomfortable vacuum about what values the organization stands by and what the strategy is.' It was a powerful demonstration of how a huge effort to instil values can be subverted by top managers failing to model the right behaviour.[6]

Important though modelling is, unless the issue is particularly high profile, as happened in the Citigroup case, the audience present when ethical dilemmas arise is often quite small. Consequently, the modelled behaviour may be missed by the majority of employees who are engaged with activities elsewhere. This is why it is important that leaders find ways to multiply the effectiveness of modelling. They can set the stage in advance and make sure that the examples are widely circulated and that people discuss observed behaviour that models good ethical conduct.

Leadership on the line

Since leadership behaviour fundamentally influences the development of ethical conduct, two important questions arise: 'Will I be a champion, an exemplar or both?' and 'How do I perform either role?'

If you are a senior leader, such as head of a business division, in the top management team or even the CEO, others will normally expect you to be both champion and exemplar. As a middle or first-line manager, or a supervisor, employees will look most directly to you for help on ethical matters, rather than seniors far away in a corporate office.

While you can task others with the role of champion, you cannot escape the responsibility of the exemplar role. Unless people see you modelling the right behaviour, you will be undermining the ethical programme, even if that is not your intention.

To be an exemplar, there are five main practical tasks to focus on: demonstrate that ethics are a priority, communicate clear expectations for ethical practice, promote ethical decision making, support your local ethics programme, and take vigorous action against unethical practices. Each has detailed implications for daily activity (see the box on page 141).

To model that ethics is a priority

- Tell your staff to make ethics a priority.
- Use examples of stories from your experience and area of responsibility.
- Initiate discussions of ethical concerns.
- In a typical day, be seen to think about and talk about ethics.
- Demonstrate that you are sensitive to ethical issues in your everyday work.
- Explicitly acknowledge staff contributions to supporting ethical practices.
- Hold your staff responsible for meeting high ethical standards.[7]

Start by paying regular attention to ethics. Let people see you taking the issue seriously. When this happens frequently, the result will tend to show up as less unethical behaviour, fewer situations inviting ethical misconduct, and higher levels of overall employee satisfaction with the organization.

Second, if you want others to do the right ethical thing – you need to offer practical ways to do this. This means both speaking the ethics message and avoiding inappropriate behaviours, and regularly highlighting and rewarding ethical performance. For example, when you encounter someone dealing successfully with a significant ethical dilemma, consider how to publicize and celebrate this, so that others in the organization get to hear about it. (See the box on page 143 on doing the right thing.)

Two role models for ethical practice

Model 1:

- Project professionalism and responsibility at all times.
- Demonstrate respect and consideration for others.
- Maintain composure and poise even in times of crisis.
- Act in an honest, forthright, and trustworthy way.
- Treat everyone fairly and do not play to favourites.
- Follow through on promises and commitments.
- Exercise self-control and restraint.
- Choose to take the 'high road' even when others do not.

Model 2:

General Mills – from: A Champion's Code of Conduct

Chances are you will find yourself faced with an ethical dilemma. This is especially true if you manage a team. You know that perception matters, candour is critical, and the answers are not always as clear as you would hope. You also know that we are all accountable to the company and to each other. To maintain high ethical standards, you should:

- *Show what it means to act with integrity.*
- *Operate in an honest and candid manner.*
- *Create an open environment that invites engagement.*
- *Ensure those you supervise understand and act according to General Mills' policies and expectations.*
- *Emphasize that help is available if it's needed.*
- *Know about available resources when issues are identified.*
- *Support employees who in good faith ask questions or raise concerns.*
- *Report instances of noncompliance with the law, our policies or this Code.*

© General Mills. Reprinted with permission

Third, what a leader does *not* do also sends a powerful message. For example, you are saying loud and clear that ethics are not a high priority if you skip ethics-related items on meeting agendas, decline requests for resources to support ethics activities or are conspicuously absent from events in the local ethics programme. (See box below.)

Since 2004, Illinois state employees have been required by the State Officials and Employees Ethics Act to undergo annual ethics training. The training is conducted online or in person and takes about 40 minutes to an hour to complete. Every year about 99.9 per cent of the university's around 49,000 employees comply with the requirement.

Van den Dries, a professor in charge of a maths department, was reportedly reminded many times to complete the training, by university administrators, including the then Chancellor. Apparently he dismissed state ethics training, reportedly branding it 'Orwellian', and was subsequently fined $500 for not completing it several years in a row. According to local news reports, after years of refusing to do so he eventually accepted the fine and took the online ethics training.

There are numerous other ways for leaders to be a champion or an exemplar. For example, in your normal role you probably attend performance reviews or expect to see the results of those held by direct reports. Show that ethics matter by your insistence that all reviews include specific expectations for ethical practice in staff performance plans. The review documentation should confirm that the topic was discussed and the person's performance assessed for their commitment to ethical behaviour and the company's core values.

Another way to be a champion or exemplar is to use your authority to free up staff to support the ethics programme. This could involve making it clear that you sanction their attendance at relevant meetings about ethical matters. You can also encourage your people to come forward as ethics champions, confirming that their time spent doing this will not be seen as detracting from their daily work.

Rewarding staff for contributing to ethical practice is further evidence of your credentials as champion or exemplar (see also Chapter 6 on systems and procedures). The issue of rewards has long been a contentious one for companies. While some people argue that it is wrong to reward people for simply 'doing the right thing', the more compelling evidence from psychological research shows that rewarding behaviour encourages more of it. Consequently, you can build ethics and other values into non-cash reward programmes. An outstanding and courageous demonstration of ethics, such as blowing the whistle on a suspicious accounting practice or suggesting a novel approach to safeguarding confidential data, can be award-worthy in a recognition programme with significant non-cash rewards.[8]

Sometimes being a champion or exemplar comes down to readily responding when people raise ethical issues during their daily work. For example, you can seek assurance that there has been effective follow-through on these matters by demanding progress reports and showing interest in the results.

Doing the right thing

Case 1

If managers model the right behaviour, subordinates will probably do the same. This was the message that senior management sent to lower-level managers and supervisors throughout Martin Marietta, a leading producer of construction components.

The company was engaged in a tough competitive battle over a major contract. Because both Martin Marietta and its main competitor were qualified to do the work, the job would go to the lower bid. A few days before bids were due, a package arrived at Martin Marietta. It contained a copy of the competitor's bid sheet. This potentially invaluable intelligence probably came from a disgruntled employee trying to sabotage their employer's efforts. The bid price was lower than Martin Marietta's.

In a display of ethical backbone, executives immediately turned the envelope over to the government and informed the competitor. They did not change their own bid in the meantime, nor did they win the job. All they got was a memorable opportunity to send a clear ethical message to the entire organization.[9]

Case 2

The CEO of a large company discovered that some of his employees were checking the rubbish outside a competitor's offices – sifting for information to give them a competitive advantage. The manager running the espionage operation was a personal friend of the CEO's, but he was immediately fired, as were his 'operatives'.

The CEO informed his competitor about the venture and returned all the materials that had been gathered. Like the managers in Case 1 above, this executive modelled ethical behaviour, sending a clear message to his organization: namely, departures from accepted behaviour would not be tolerated.[10]

Case 3

When Lucent Technologies found that managers in its Chinese operations bribed government officials in order to do business there, the company fired its entire senior management team in China. While this way of doing business may be common in China, it is illegal in the United States.[11]

Major UK retail food chain

Maria is Head of Responsible Trading in charge of setting and monitoring the working conditions standards for all the factories and farms producing the company's food, across 30 sourcing countries. She and her colleagues have organized and chaired numerous conferences across the world for more than 900 of the company's suppliers to help them enact ethical trade practices throughout the supply chain.

For Maria, the formal auditing process can only ever be part of the answer of achieving ethical practice. One such conference had a huge effect on a supplier who was repeatedly failing to meet the company's ethical trading standards, despite frequent offers of advice, help and resources. In a last attempt to resolve the issue, Maria invited the supplier to a conference, to listen to other suppliers talking about issues they faced and how they had resolved them. She recalls the suppliers' reaction to the conference as 'having their eyes opened'.

Hearing how other people had resolved their issues, the supplier in question was left feeling embarrassed that they were not looking after their own workforce. She describes how they went home and spent all night reading the company's workbook and deciding what they needed to do. After a frantic week of fast action, she reveals, 'they had moved heaven and earth, and their factory was a completely different place'.[12]

UK supermarket chain

This supermarket chain appoints ethical champions and has 40 of them across the UK and its international businesses. Many hold technical roles and are ideally placed to take a strategic view of supplier management and ongoing developments.

According to the company's published material, its ethical champions in each commercial category are volunteers with a normal day job who have an interest in standards. They reportedly help their teams review decisions, prepare monthly reports and follow up corrective action plans and any other concerns at individual sites. In its publicly available documents the company reveals that a member of its central Ethical Trading Team also meets with each category ethical champion to discuss progress. The main board commercial director also reviews aggregate audit data every four weeks, and discusses any concerns with the relevant commercial directors and the ethical trade manager.[13]

New Look

New Look, a leading UK fashion retailer, expects its buyers in commercial teams to have a key role in supporting its policy of trading fairly. According to its published reports, ethical champions were introduced into the buying team on a voluntary basis to help build understanding of workers' issues throughout the team. The volunteer ethical champions come from different levels and functions across the group. They act as ambassadors for ethical trade throughout the business and are enthusiastic advocates for ethical trade, spreading the word in their day jobs.[14]

Sasol

Sasol is an integrated energy and chemicals company based in South Africa. The Group Ethics Office is the custodian of the company's ethics strategy and consists of just five people. There are 50 ethics officers around the world who help implement the ethics programme across this diverse, multinational company.

Every managing director of every business unit and head of function appoints an ethics officer, who must be a person of integrity who reports to the MD. Ethics champions are then appointed by the ethics officers, who help them in their duties. The collective mission is to encourage compliance with various laws, 'but more importantly encourage each employee and champion to adhere to the highest standards of ethical behaviour as set forth in the goals of Sasol's Ethics code'.

The ethics officers sign a pledge which makes clear what is expected of them. It sets out the mission, the officer's duties and other important information about the role: 'I solemnly pledge that I will abide by Sasol's Code of Ethics and that I will always endeavour to fulfil my role as an ethics officer or champion with responsibility, honesty, fairness and respect. I understand that Sasol's value of Integrity is integral to Sasol's Code of Ethics.'

Ethics officers have a real responsibility with specific deliverables and not merely to quietly support ethics in the background. Ethics officers are encouraged to appoint ethics champions to assist them in fulfilling their duties. Ethics champions often help with 'investigations' – looking into the allegations that were received through the company's whistleblowing line and checking the validity of the allegations. Most ethics champions also attend ethics training where they meet their fellow champions and the Group Ethics Office.

ACTION POINTERS

- Organize a systematic search to locate the company's ethical champions.
- If possible, bring all champions together to generate a critical mass to affect the culture.
- Be alert to resorting to mental gymnastics – mind games that undermine the ethics message.

- As a senior leader you will need to be both a champion and an exemplar.

- Exercise moral courage by facing up to ethical dilemmas and moral wrongdoing – your people expect it.

- Find ways to multiply the effectiveness of modelling the right behaviour by making sure that examples are widely circulated and discussed.

- To build your credentials as an ethical champion, start by paying close attention to ethics, let people see you taking the issue seriously.

- Readily speak about ethics and avoid inappropriate behaviours which could undermine it.

- Regularly highlight and reward ethical performance.

- Things not to do include: don't skip ethics-related items on meetings agendas, or decline requests for resources to support the ethics initiative, or fail to attend local ethics programme events.

- Show that ethics matter to you by insisting that all reviews include specific expectations for ethical practice in staff performance plans.

- Seek confirmation reviews by direct reports and include an ethics-related item.

- Use your authority to free up staff to support the ethics programme.

- Sanction your people's attendance at relevant meetings about ethical matters.

- Reward staff for contributing to ethical practice through recognition programmes and non-cash rewards.

- Seek assurance that there has been effective follow-through when people raise ethical issues from their daily work.

- Communicate ethics as a priority and provide people with regular information about what is going on in developing the ethical culture.

Notes

1 This extract comes from the company's Statement of Ethics: Leading with Integrity in Wal-Mart. However, this company's business practices have been criticized for forcing down wages and sending well-paying jobs overseas. It has been accused of violating labour laws. Community groups, grassroots organizations, religious organizations and environmental groups have all protested the company's policies and business practices at various times

2 Chartered Institute of Management Accountants (2010) Incorporating ethics into strategy: developing sustainable business models, Discussion paper, February

3 Kerns, C (2003) Why good leaders do bad things, mental gymnastics behind unethical behaviour, *Graziardo Business Review*, **6** (4)

4 Treanor, J (2012) Barclays 'will be about values, not just value', *Guardian*, 14 September

5 American Management Association (2006) The ethical enterprise: doing the right things in the right ways, today and tomorrow: a global study of business ethics 2005–2015

6 Persaud, A and Plender, J (2006) The day Dr Evil wounded a financial giant, *Financial Times*, 23 August

7 See, for example, US Department of Veterans Affairs (2007) Integrated Ethics: Ethics leadership toolkit: a manual for the ethical leadership coordinator, Washington, DC

8 Mitchell, C *et al* (2005) Rewarding ethical behaviour, originally published in *workspan*, the magazine of WorldatWork, July

9 Episode recounted by Norm Augustine, 'Business ethics in the 21st century' (speech, Ethics Resource Center), http://www.ethics.org/resources/speech_detail.cfm?ID=848

10 Augustine, N (2006) Business ethics in the 21st century, Ethics Resource Center, 24 April

11 Chen, R and Chen, C-P (2005) Chinese professional managers and the issue of ethical behaviour, *Business Journal*, Global Business, May/June

12 See, for example, Ethical trade initiative, http://www.ethicaltrade.org/in-action/people/louise-nicholls

13 Step-by-step guide to reviewing and improving purchasing practices (2010) Ethical Trade Initiative

14 Leaving a legacy. A new look at our ethics (2009) New Look Group

PART THREE
Individual requirements

Learning: Will and skill

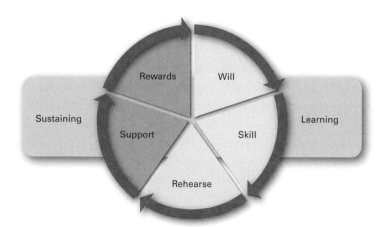

09

EXECUTIVE SUMMARY

- People often need help understanding the relevance of business ethics; it starts with the leadership setting the tone.
- After announcing the importance of ethics and distributing the rules, leaders often think the job's done.
- Clarify what a successful training outcome will look like.
- Many companies train people in business ethics; 90 per cent completion rates are common.
- Effective training builds skills in recognizing and solving ethical dilemmas.
- Employees who undergo ethics training expect to see evidence that their leaders value this learning effort.
- Ethics training is cost-effective, particularly if it prevents serious reputational damage.
- Most leaders will benefit from their own ethics and values 'tune-up'.
- When promoting ethical behaviour, leaders must provide convincing answers to 'What's in it for me?' for each person.

Will

Even the most rational approach to ethics is defenceless if there isn't the will to do what is right. ALEXANDER SOLZHENITSYN, **RUSSIAN NOVELIST, HISTORIAN AND NOBEL PRIZE-WINNER**

If you lead a public relations company you will probably have your own views on what it means to be ethical. More than most business leaders, PR executives face tests every day as to whether and how to spin their messages. For many critics, spin is blatantly unethical, so it is hardly surprising that PR experts have suggested that companies in this field not only need a general definition of what it means to be ethical, they also need the 'will to be ethical'. You are perhaps not in the PR business, but whether your people have the will to be ethical plays an important part in the development of an ethical culture. How, then, do you develop the will to be ethical in others?

People like change. They don't much like being changed. Leaders who attempt to alter ethical behaviour must offer powerful reasons for why each person should act differently. For example, one route to achieving change is through the fear factor. This might take the form of telling people that their jobs are at risk if they break certain rules. Fear of retribution, though, tends to produce diminishing returns. The more you do it, the less effective it becomes. Fear does not make people receptive to training, and worse, they will not necessarily be compliant when it comes to speaking up about ethical issues.

An alternative route to winning individual behaviour change is offering an attraction rather than a threat. For example, making it clear that people can gain promotion, personal recognition or some other benefit for doing what's right. The downside is that attraction may blur the boundaries between what is acceptable and not acceptable behaviour.

Neither fear nor attraction makes much sense alone. What works best is some combination of both. When it comes to behaving ethically, leaders must find ways to provide each person with a convincing answer to 'What's in it for me?' It must appeal to what motivates them, such as a sense of community, contributing to society, having a worthwhile shared purpose, living their own values, a vision of a desired future and so on.

A compelling reason why people alter their behaviour is from a sense of urgency, such as fresh oversight of their actions, and changed management priorities. Equally persuasive may be compelling stories of what happened when things went wrong and employees violated standards. For instance, those in professional services usually readily identify with the drama of the rapid demise of Arthur Andersen, due to unethical practices. Or trainers might develop a 'disaster parade' of headlines about enterprises and individuals who have been prosecuted or held liable for misconduct.

Voicing values

Employees who are in touch with their own values find it easier to align with what matters to the company. Therefore helping them articulate their values makes sense. The intention cannot be to alter their values, but rather to understand and relate them to the company's declared values. Leaders can adopt various methods of affecting people's willingness to try to be ethical:[1]

- Giving voice: this develops employees' ability and confidence to voice their values and concerns, rather than mainly relying on rules and policies to supply the answer to the question: 'What is the right thing to do?'

- Shared stories: the power of storytelling for building a shared culture is well established. The more real these stories are, the more likely it is that they will have a positive impact on people's attitude towards being willing to tackle ethical issues at work.

- Use individual strengths: rather than exhorting people to be bolder, this method helps people reframe their values conflicts so that acting on them appears safer than not doing so.

- Pre-scripting: give people a form of script setting out responses to values conflicts. People practise using scripts in informal settings such as team meetings, and in formal training sessions to try out how to speak about an ethical situation, for example saying reasons for not acting on one's values. Together employees craft persuasive responses and practise delivering them.

- Peer coaching: use formal and informal coaching opportunities for people to try out scripts, arguments and descriptions of ethical dilemmas (see also Chapter 10).

Skill

'We will never experience this again', declared Novo Nordisk, the Danish pharma company. This followed a hefty fine for making improper payments to the former Iraqi government of Saddam Hussein. Later it launched a training programme across its multinational group to make sure that everyone worked to the company's business ethics and guidelines.

Colleagues in some countries protested. They complained that it disadvantaged them, making them the only company in their country required to act in this way. 'We had some turbulence,' revealed HR Director Lise Kingo, 'until our CEO stood up and said, on several occasions, that we only want business when it lives up to our business ethics guidelines – otherwise forget about it. That was very powerful.'[2]

As the Novo Nordisk experience shows, people often need help to understand the relevance of business ethics. It starts with the leadership setting the tone. Leaders first make clear to everyone that ethics matter. Next, there is a real effort to develop new learning, through actions such as ethics training. When Citigroup wanted to change its then unethical trading culture, it began with one of the most thorough training exercises and ethics courses in financial services. Sadly, though, this was torpedoed by Citigroup's managers who failed to tackle actual cases of unethical practices.

'Business ethics' can be interpreted in so many ways. For example, the Swedish bank Svenska Handelsbanken AB sees a competitive advantage in going back to the ethics of old-style banking. Caterpillar Inc sees business ethics as having strong goals and strategies committed to sustainability and the environment.

For everyday purposes, business ethics means standards of behaviour – of individuals, not just the business as a whole. Each company and industry needs to develop its own view of what acting ethically means, and identify the specific skills its stakeholders require. An ethical business environment emerges mainly through observable individual behaviour, such as: maintains confidentiality; is truthful; confronts potentially unethical behaviour; does not look the other way; avoids conflicts of interest; deals fairly with customers.

Developing people's skills

Check out any major company and somewhere you will probably find a statement of its business principles. Sometimes these apply worldwide, as in the case of BT with its five business behaviour fundamentals in every country in which it operates. These refer to acting legally, competing fairly, dealing with inducements, handling conflicts and making commitments. Other companies make a more local interpretation – the 'do as they do in Rome' approach.

Leaders often convince themselves that the job's done, having issued the company's values, rules or written codes. But while making speeches and distributing written materials are necessary, they are not enough. Everyone in the company, from senior managers to the most junior employee, needs time at work to make sense of the company's business standards and expectations. 'What does responsible business conduct mean?', for example, and 'How does our compliance system work?', 'How do I deal with an ethical dilemma when it happens?' They also need guidance on developing ethical awareness, for instance, 'What are our roles and responsibilities?'

Your company may therefore need to prime its ethical moral compass using a wide variety of means, including tailored training sessions. For instance, you may want training mainly to help avoid adverse publicity, potential lawsuits, illegal behaviour, and monetary and criminal penalties. A 2003 study by the Ethics Resource Center found that the higher the number of ethics programme elements in place, the more likely employees were to report misconduct.

Or you may direct your ethical training to win a strategic advantage – customers and employees prefer companies with a commitment to being ethical. Some of the best-known early examples are Body Shop with its ethic against animal testing; Ben & Jerry's ice creams with its 'reduce, reuse, and recycle' approach; and M&S with its commitment to sustainability and 'no plan B'. More recently, Primark has created an Ethical Trade Manager position in Bangladesh whose early initiative has been to launch tailored ethical training for suppliers there.

Ethics training may sound like a luxury, but many companies conclude that it's a better alternative to paying legal fees arising from bad business practices. For example, the Ethics and Compliance group and the Legal Department of US health-care company Baxters conducted over 400 class-room sessions around the world in 2011, training a total of 13,844 employees on its ethics and compliance standards and supporting policies.

Participants should leave the training:

- aware of the likely consequences of unethical behaviour;
- confident about what the company expects from them;
- able to recognize issues of responsible business conduct and have the confidence – and courage – to make the right decision;
- able to explain their ethical choices to the appropriate people;
- understanding why the business ethics programme matters to the company as a whole;

- convinced that they will not be punished if they make a mistake but can demonstrate they followed the agreed decision-making process.

Achieving these results through training was once regarded as best practice. Now it's commonplace. Completion rates, for instance, are now widely expected to reach over 90 per cent. A one-off training event, though, is fairly useless and a poor investment. It is simply going through the motions. Nor will training alone make a major difference to ethical behaviour.[3] Only a continuous effort will keep people constantly alert to ethical concerns. In fact, the best organizations go beyond completion rates and the basic training investment. They try to instil the underlying values of an ethical business culture.

Companies may adopt additional ways to strengthen people's ethical skills, using follow-up testing, random spot checks, helplines, regular newsletters and so on. They also recognize that sometimes the best solution is highly bespoke training. This might include 'train the trainers' workshops, a board-level ethics workshop and one-to-one board mentoring.

Effective training builds employee skills in ethical awareness – the ability to recognize an ethical dilemma and use a systematic approach to sorting it. Once people become aware of the implications of ethical behaviour, they are more likely to draw on their personal values to make sense of the company's code of behaviour. In the case of managers, it may include practice at talking about difficult ethical issues. For example, a retired chief ethics officer in the global security company Northrop Grumman established a programme giving managers practice at having unpleasant conversations about ethics, and ethical performance, without being hurtful. Such exercises are increasingly common in large corporations.

Creating the necessary ethical mindfulness is part of the challenge of devising an effective training or learning experience. For example, training is often concentrated on compliance, making sure you do what you are supposed to do. But there is considerable evidence to suggest that what works better is training that focuses on integrity – doing what you know to be right.

A study of 10,000 employees in six US companies in a variety of industries[4] found strong evidence that integrity programmes outperform compliance programmes and produce:

- lower incidence of unethical/illegal behaviour;

- greater awareness of the existence of ethical and legal issues;

- a stronger search for ethical advice;

- more willingness to deliver bad news to management;

- more reporting on ethics violations;

- more ethics and compliance embedded into decision making;

- greater employee commitment to the firm.

Few decisions symbolize your leadership commitment to the company's ethics programme more than insisting that people regularly devote time for training in responsible business conduct. Similarly, rescheduling busy day-to-day operations to accommodate regular employee training conveys an important message from managers and supervisors. It underlines the intention to take seriously standards, procedures and expectations. Where ethics training becomes an integral part of how the company operates – its normal culture – employees tend to value it more than where it's treated as an irritant or necessary evil.

Designing the ethics training

Designing a training programme requires as much focus on objectives and outcomes as the design of the business ethics programme as a whole. The training programme should be based on the company's core beliefs. It must reflect the pressures on the company and its organizational culture.

This means taking account of the situation, the resources available, the business activities, participants, target audiences and expected outcomes. Without this attention to detail, neither the business ethics programme nor training will be easy to evaluate. How will you know what success looks like? Examples of aims are:

- Make a positive contribution toward making the ethics programme succeed.

- Ensure we have the right people, in the right places, to run an ethical business.

- Employees understand the codes, standards and procedures and can explain what's expected of them.

- Know what stakeholders expect of us when mistakes, misconduct or misunderstandings occur involving our standards and procedures.

- Make certain that our vendors understand the implications for them of the company's business ethics.

- Build employees' skills in handling ethical dilemmas and resisting unethical behaviour, and ensure that they understand where to seek advice and support.

- Help all employees make the connection between ethical business practices and the company's core values and business aims.

- Convey management's sincere desire to know whether its standards and procedures are being followed.

- Meet specific legal requirements for employees to have a working knowledge of relevant issues, laws, regulations, and standards of ethics, compliance and responsibility.

In 2003, Tesco made ethical trade training compulsory for all commercial staff. Peter Grove, a Tesco UK category director in non-foods, found the experience 'terrifying' but tremendously useful: 'Now, when I'm in a factory with my technical manager, while I may not always know what I'm looking for to the same extent as him, I have the confidence to pipe up and question something if I think it looks a bit suspect.'

After the training, Grove's whole perspective on his work changed. 'Now, when I look at a product, I think: that's a great product, where has it come from? Does it look labour intensive or machine-made? What are conditions in the factory like, not just how can we beat our competitors with this product?'[5]

Don't send a video

Employees who undergo ethics training expect to see evidence that their leaders value this learning effort. They will need to see leaders supporting the training through actions, and not just by their words. For example, simply sending a video from the CEO saying how important business ethics are can be a sure way to sow seeds of doubt about the real value attached to the activity.

Instead, leaders, managers and supervisors should put in personal appearances to affirm their commitment to the programme. This works even better if they appear and observe training under way, and make themselves available to answer questions. Employees are unlikely to value training that senior management does not appear to support.

Is training cost-effective?

Even the most enthusiastic leaders who favour running an ethical business may wonder whether training people to handle ethical issues is worthwhile. What are the true gains and are these justified in pure business terms, apart from being 'the right thing to do'?

If training achieves the major goals set for it, such as helping to avoid serious reputational damage, then almost certainly it is cost-effective. When people gain new knowledge about ethical issues, they also acquire confidence to deal with them properly, often saving the company serious damage. However, the nature of training matters. If it's too narrow, tackling, say, just handling codes of practice, it may do little to develop useful day-to-day skills. Also, the methods for communicating the learning need to be varied, aimed at stimulating people's interest. For example, Baker Hughes, a petroleum company, takes a wide-ranging approach to this kind of development, involving continuous improvement, shared accountability and transparency (see Figure 9.1).

For the investment in ethics training to be worthwhile, it's essential to select the best way to develop people's skills. Suppose you want employees to recognize an issue of responsible business conduct when they come across it. If so, then training consisting mainly of written information, on-screen instructions or talk and chalk lectures will almost certainly fail. Unless employees have live practice at addressing ethical issues, they are unlikely to develop the skill and confidence to tackle them in the real work situation.

Training can also help employees avoid false reasoning to justify unethical behaviour. For example, people often convince themselves that an activity is not illegal or immoral. Or they tell themselves that some wrong action is actually in the best interest of the individual or the corporation. Or they decide that it will never be found out. A typical rationalization or false reasoning is assuming that the company will condone some wrong behaviour because it will help the company achieve an important goal, such as winning a major contract. If training develops understanding about, and resistance to, such rationalizations, the investment in learning will almost certainly be worth it.

Yet another benefit from the investment in ethical training is to provide feedback on whether the overall ethics programme is working well. It has the capability to uncover sensitive matters, such as insufficient guidance for employees on ethical dilemmas, unreasonable stakeholder expectations, unresolved legal issues, unfair treatment of employees, difficult working conditions.

FIGURE 9.1 Baker Hughes' approach to communication: continuous improvement, shared accountability and transparency

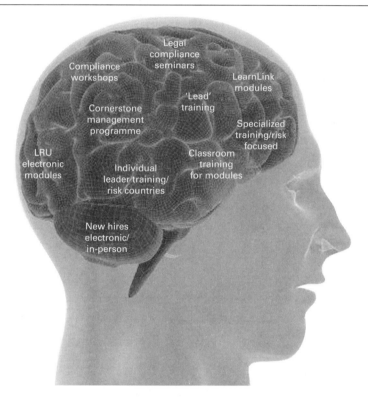

Legal
compliance
seminars

Compliance
workshops

LearnLink
modules

'Lead'
training

Cornerstone
management
programme

Specialized
training/risk
focused

LRU
electronic
modules

Classroom
training
for modules

Individual
leader training/
risk countries

New hires
electronic/
in-person

SOURCE: Azeez, T *et al* (2008) Good ethics makes good business sense, Baker Hughes Inc, International Petroleum Technology Conference held in Kuala Lumpur, Malaysia, 3–5 December. Reproduced with permission.

Boeing

According to the company's own published material, some 145,000 employees have been exposed to its ethics value programme, in a customized in-house programme tailored to meet the organization's ethics goals. Employees reportedly receive a company-created pamphlet entitled 'Business Conduct Guidelines', which stresses policies on ethics and standards of conduct and compliance; hypothetical situations are presented, and a business ethics adviser in each division leads discussions. The training is also said to stress the procedures for discussing or reporting unethical behaviour or infractions.

Regardless of lofty credos and top management pronouncements, the company will need robust mechanisms for translating ethics principles into meaningful actions. Whatever their area of responsibility, every employee must come to understand what ethics mean in practice. Specifically, each person should feel confident that their chosen course of action reflects the organization's ethical standards and its core values, and will be supported by the organization.

Generally, training to achieve this will have more impact on middle and junior employees than on more senior employees. For example, research by the Ethics Research Center found that 79 per cent of non-managers who had been trained felt ready to handle risk (Figure 9.2). This compared to 58 per cent of non-managers who had not been trained. This 21 percentage point gap is highly significant. In an era where funds for training in ethics are likely to be scarce, the available resources should probably be targeted at first-line supervisors and non-managers.

FIGURE 9.2   Percent who feel prepared to handle risk situations

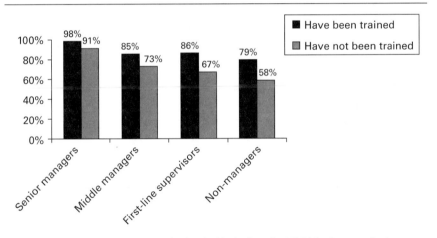

SOURCE: Critical elements of an organizational ethical culture (2006) Ethics Resource Center

© 2012 Ethics Resource Center. Used with permission of the Ethics Resource Center, 2345 Crystal Drive, Ste 201, Arlington, VA 22202, www.ethics.org

Can't it all be done online?

Whatever training approach your company adopts, it is important to avoid ethics fatigue. This occurs when the ethics messages are badly presented or people have too much exposure to them. Sitting at a screen, no matter how animated or visual the messages, eyes soon glaze over. Since the amount of ethics training available is often extremely small – perhaps only one to three hours per employee per year, educational fatigue might seem unlikely. Yet it happens when there is over-reliance on computer-based methods. By themselves, these seldom deliver a sufficiently stimulating or sustained impact to affect actual behaviour. The answer is a blended approach using multiple formats throughout the year that engages employees' interest in ethical choices.

Some of the most effective ways are those created by Levi Strauss, American Express, Campbell Soup Company and Tyco. These give people techniques for solving ethical dilemmas. They are presented with a series of situations and asked to come up with the best ethical solution. To add excitement, companies use quizzes, interactive games, simulations, action learning sets, podcasts, role play, psycho drama and so on. Citigroup, for example, created a board game, The Work Ethic. Players strive to correctly answer ethics questions involving legal, regulatory, policy-related and judgement issues. Other companies use multimedia, including a daily newsletter, ethics crossword puzzles, videos and even a film festival.

Tyco

Tyco is a leader in fire protection, security and life safety, with global headquarters in Switzerland. The company gained notoriety during the early 2000s. Since then, the company has undergone major changes and still has 70,000 employees worldwide, a drop from the 240,000 employed at the time of the scandal.

In 2009, the company reportedly conducted a cultural survey to discover what its employees thought of ethics and compliance. It seems that there was both good and bad news. Given the history at the top of the company, there was strong support for ethics and compliance. But things were different in the lower reaches. Support for ethics and compliance was said to be much softer. As one senior manager reportedly said, it was 'a wake-up call'.[6]

An independent ethics publication describes how the compliance team brainstormed: How do we reach this audience? They brought in outside vendors to make presentations. Firms offered board games that could be played to reinforce the ethics message. They suggested card games and other creative learning devices. But these alternatives were expensive and the group was unimpressed by them.

Instead, they said 'Let's keep it simple.' They settled on a model borrowed from the corporate safety area, 'toolbox talks'. In some organizations, managers deliver a safety talk about a specific subject at the beginning of the work shift. These can be done in a variety of ways, but they typically consist of a brief two- to five-minute interactive discussion. Tyco launched The Ethical Reflection Programme in which, every quarter, managers would pick up a scenario from the company's Ethics Reflections Website. They launched a conversation with their team during a regular, planned meeting, not a special compliance meeting.

SOURCES: Company published sources and correspondence with Tyco

Leaders need help too

Leaders have a tough time these days convincing us that they are honest. A US survey in 2011, for example, found that nearly half (48 per cent) of those questioned rated the honesty and ethics of CEOs as low.[7] Of equal concern is that only a tiny proportion of all major companies (3 per cent) reach high ethical standards. That is, few have developed their values into a moral compass pointing the way to comprehensive trading policies, robust structures and systems, and many other elements contributing to running an ethical business.

In trying to shift their cultures towards a more ethical approach, many leaders will conclude that they too need to develop their own skills in handling ethics. For example, some may neglect to ensure the nuts and bolts of what makes an ethics programme effective. This is seldom due to negligence, but to lack of awareness of what it takes to make a sustained cultural change in the right direction. Consequently, many leaders will benefit from having their own ethics and values tune-up. This includes opportunities to examine their own ethical decision-making skills and the ethical environment of the company.

Is it an ethical dilemma?

Warning signs that you are facing an ethical problem include feelings of:

- Discomfort – if something about a situation makes you uneasy, it is time to start finding out what is causing the feeling and why.
- Guilt – rather than deny the feeling, explore and respond to it.
- Stress – putting off making a difficult choice, losing sleep and feeling pressured can all be signs of an ethical problem.

- Anger – if you are feeling angry at being pressured, it could be a sign of an ethical problem.

- Embarrassment – if you would feel awkward about telling your boss, co-workers, friends or family about what you are doing, or thinking of doing, it's a good chance that the issue is an ethical one.

- Fear – if you're afraid of being caught, found out or exposed for what you are doing or thinking of doing, it's almost certainly an ethical matter.

Training can help managers clarify their ethical framework and practise self-discipline when making decisions in difficult circumstances. According to the London-based Institute of Business Ethics, which surveys UK companies every three years on the use of their codes of ethics, six out of ten UK companies provided training in business ethics for all their staff in 2010. However, this is a 10 per cent drop on 2007. 'Although we are living in a time of austerity, cutting back on ethics training is a short-sighted thing for companies to do', comments Simon Webley, Research Director of the IBE and author of the survey.

ACTION POINTERS

- Develop clarity about what acting ethically means for your company and what specific skills stakeholders require.

- Offer your people guidance and training in developing ethical reasoning, and their roles and responsibilities.

- Get really clear about the aims of any ethical training programme – what outcomes do you want, what will success look like?

- Demand evidence that people leave training confident that they know what the company expects of them.

- See that training gives people skills in recognizing an ethical dilemma and how to adopt a systematic approach for tackling it.

- Aim to make ethics training an integral part of how the company operates.

- Be willing to put in a personal appearance at training sessions to affirm the leadership's commitment to the learning programme and its core messages.

- Consider whether you and fellow leaders would benefit from your own ethics and values 'tune-up'.

- Develop convincing reasons why people need to undertake training that answers their unspoken question 'What's in it for me?'

Notes

1 See, for example, Gentile, M (2011) Combating ethical cynicism and voicing values in the workplace, *Ivy Business Journal*, June

2 Smedley, T (2011) On my agenda, *People Management*, September

3 Ethics Resource Center (2006) Critical elements of an organizational ethical culture

4 Treviño, L *et al* (1999) Managing ethics and legal compliance: what works and what hurts, *California Management Review*, **41** (2), 131–51

5 Ethical Trading Initiatives (2008) Communication strategies: get buy-in, Workshop 1, ETI Conference 2008: the next decade

6 *Ethikos* magazine (May/June 2010), http://www.ethikospublication.com/html/tyco.html

7 Public Affairs Council (2011) Public Affairs Pulse Survey: What Americans think about business, Washington, DC

10 Learning: Rehearse

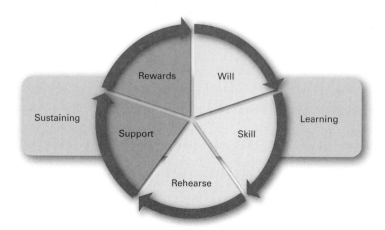

EXECUTIVE SUMMARY

- There is strong evidence from many disciplines that rehearsal is a vital way that people learn, including about ethical dilemmas.

- It is sometimes difficult to recognize an ethical issue, even when it is right in front of you.

- Experiential learning creates a highly interactive approach in which learners become mentally and emotionally involved in a 'real' ethical dilemma.

- Experiential learning has a far greater impact than more familiar methods such as lectures, discussion sessions or online tuition.

- 'Immersive' technology takes rehearsal to a new level of reality, adding more realism and further engaging individuals.

- Drama-based means for creating rehearsal conditions are only effective when they stimulate human interactions and produce a sustained learning result.

- If the rehearsal meets certain criteria it is likely to be a visceral experience – something you 'feel' in your body, not just your mind.

- The right form of rehearsal creates opportunities for people to use all of themselves, to shift fairly painlessly from one sort of behaviour to another.

'I think 20 tons have fallen from my shoulders. I prepared for this for seven years', said Felix Baumgartner after making history in October 2012, skydiving from a distance of 23 miles and being the first person to break the sound barrier outside of a vehicle. But he didn't do it alone, nor was it a casual one-off affair.

With a complete team behind him, he conducted endless rehearsals and checks, in which he did numerous run-throughs, practising using the space suit, the capsule, managing the balloon, the cameras and the communications. Just before the actual jump, fearless Felix even did a couple of high-altitude dress rehearsals, leaping from 96,640 ft – just 6,000 ft shy of a world record set in 1960 by Joe Kittinger, a US Air Force test pilot.

When you work on an oil rig, they don't just hand you a book of safety rules and say: 'Watch out for the dangers.' You practise helicopter escape, personal survival, using life crafts, first aid post-evacuation, fire-fighting, and putting on and controlling breathing apparatus. Your survival may depend on being able to do these tasks, not just acquire an intellectual understanding of what they involve.

If you're a frequent flyer you'll be familiar with the airline crew standing in the middle of the cabin going through the safety routines. Sometimes this routine information comes as a short video or even a cartoon. You may or may not watch it with your full attention. This is training, not rehearsal. If you actually had to do any of the safety actions for real, you almost certainly would not feel entirely confident about any of it.

No amount of teaching, training or development substitutes for actually doing a new task. Whether it's dancing on a reality show, working on an oil rig, using an oxygen mask or dealing with ethical choices at work, competence mainly stems from proper rehearsal. Pumping people full of facts will not make a behavioural difference. They need to try out actual ethical decision-making tools, to explore the implication of different courses of action, and experience the emotional tensions and feelings that ethical dilemmas invariably generate. Many companies now provide employees with actual rehearsal time – though they seldom call it that. These are among a full palette of ethics support and rewards (see Chapters 11 and 12).

As a change manager, you therefore face numerous choices of how to help people adapt to new ethical standards. The simplest approach is the abstract one of offering new meanings for old concepts – for example, introducing new rules of behaviour and giving a clear guide for judging performance. To get this message across, you walk the talk to encourage imitation and identification. You may be backed up by case materials, films, role plays and simulations. This approach is efficient, but the learning may never be fully internalized; that is, learning does not convert into normal behaviour, or become a new group norm. Consequently, employees are likely to revert to previous behaviour, once the pressure to perform lessens. Quite simply, the cultural shift probably won't be sustained – a natural entropy will occur.

If you want your people to learn to handle ethical issues, this must become part of their permanent way of being. They need to be able to scan the environment and make sense of it, arriving at their own solutions. In this approach you still expect people to adopt the new ethical behaviour, but you give them a choice of how they get there.

In designing an ethics programme, a common mistake is relying on a series of lectures. Typically, the day after a lecture participants recall less than 15 per cent of what they heard. There is also persuasive evidence that simply telling people about an issue is not enough to change their behaviour.[1]

Creating ethical conduct

One widely used approach is to create realistic scenarios of ethical dilemmas. This can give employees practice at identifying and working through the implications of resolving them. For example, a San Diego-based group purchasing organization uses a regular communication workshop to involve employees in discussions of hypothetical scenarios that employees may face.[2] Discussions increase participants' ability to scan the environment so that they can identify a potential ethical issue. Then they carefully reason through the issue, determine the possible impacts on others, ascertain the company's and individual employee's responsibilities, consider options for addressing the issue and then decide on actions to resolve it. After more than 60 workshops, employees continued to raise new considerations, identify new resources and think of novel ways to resolve issues. In addition, the discussions led employees to raise other problems that the company might face, based on their enhanced reasoning. For example, participants identified unexpected ways in which a certain action could potentially damage the company's reputation.

There is strong evidence from social psychology, decision making, heuristics, problem framing, anthropology and cognitive neuroscience that the opportunity to rehearse is not just a 'nice to have'. It's an essential way in which people learn new behaviour, experiencing what it feels like to voice ethical concerns, and integrating new behaviour into their way of working. In typical computer terms, it becomes a default setting.

Is this ethical?

An ethical dilemma at work arises when there's a conflict between two possible equally desirable or undesirable actions. It's typically where the 'rules' are unclear and with unacceptable trade-offs. For example, an employee may know something's wrong – 'it smells bad', as one approach puts it. Yet the employee may be torn between loyalty to colleagues and commitment to the company. The eventual choice will depend on developing a uniquely personal view of the world, drawing on existing formal guidance but, more significantly, also referring to individually held beliefs and desires. This is why rehearsals – the chance to practise with realistic examples or cases – is so essential for acquiring the necessary learning.

Recognizing an ethical issue can be difficult, even when right in front of you. In fact, people predict that they will behave more ethically than they actually do. When evaluating past unethical behaviour, they usually believe that they behaved more ethically than they actually did.[3] So there is a general tendency for people to fail to realize that they are making choices which affect others, with possible adverse consequences, and which should therefore be considered from a moral point of view. It is simply not a viable business strategy to claim that there is no such thing as ethics in business – this is a sure way of avoiding any personal responsibility for what is happening. If your only frame of reference for making choices is to 'make a profit', 'maximize shareholder value', 'win this sale' or 'meet the legal minimum requirements', you will almost certainly miss the ethical dimension.

At one end of the consequences spectrum, missing or avoiding the ethical dimension through lack of rehearsal may end up costing the company its reputation and even its survival. That certainly happened in the case of the demise of Arthur Andersen – there was slow yet steady erosion of ethical behaviour throughout the company that stretched over a decade or more. At the other end of the consequences spectrum, missing the ethical dimension may lead the individual or the company to do something entirely wrong morally. For example, imagine that you work for a company making cooking ovens, and you receive a visit from a government official who wants to talk about a multi-million-pound order. In discussions, you do not ask any questions about exactly why the official wants a particularly huge oven, one as a big as a large room. You focus instead on winning the order, meeting the customer's every need. Had you been morally responsible, and only slightly curious, you might have realized that the large ovens were for killing people.

Bridgestone/Firestone Inc

On 9 August 2000, Bridgestone/Firestone Inc announced that it would recall more than 6.5 million tyres. The company had become the subject of an intense federal investigation into 46 deaths and more than 300 incidents where Firestone tyres allegedly shredded on the highway.

This recall was the second biggest in history, behind only Firestone's previous recall of 14.5 million radial tyres in 1978. The 1978 tyre recall financially crippled the company for years to come and the August 2000 recall threatened to do the same. Consumers, the federal government and the press wanted to know: Why didn't Ford and Firestone recognize this problem sooner?

In my opinion, the executives missed the moral dimension when they reacted to the growing number of defective tyres as a financial concern for the company. They simply did not see it as a safety issue for their customers.

Rehearsing for real

In a leading UK accountancy firm, participants on a development programme identified their own ethical dilemmas and proceeded to act them out on the stage of the Fortune theatre, in the heart of London's West End. Their 'play' started with two accountants discussing their finding of minor evidence of dubious financial practices while auditing a client's accounts. Faced with strong pressures to complete the audit on time, the amateur actors wondered aloud whether to report the issue to the senior partner or not.

Working through the story, the two participants then acted out a second scene. In this they concluded that, even though it might throw the whole auditing timetable out, they would report the issue to a senior manager. Their small playlet showed how they would frame the issue for telling their manager about the problem they had uncovered.

There are numerous ways like this in which people rehearse dealing with real ethical dilemmas. A powerful one, like the above, is called experiential learning, sometimes also described as 'dramatic rehearsal'. It creates a highly interactive approach in which learners become mentally and emotionally involved in a 'real' ethical dilemma. The experience taps into their feelings, not just their normal logical or analytical side. It builds greater self-awareness and greater sensitivity to the situation.

In 'victim and chooser',[4] another rehearsal tool, participants may be asked what they would do if they saw a senior person acting at odds with the company's codes of practice. They then explore in depth whether their reaction would be a purely passive one – a victim, in which they complain that the choices are difficult and not for them to make – they become a 'blamer', or a 'poor me'. Or their response may be more positive – a chooser, in which they take the initiative to raise the matter through the company's telephone hotline.

By using dramatic incidents, experiential learning can push people to use their imagination to test various courses of action. In their mind they follow some impulse, for example they mentally try out some plan. In their imagination they live out the consequences that would follow. It's dramatic and active, not mathematical and impersonal. Research into affecting people's performance through training suggests that experiential learning has a far greater impact than more familiar methods such as lectures, discussions, online tuition or the provision of information.

Extreme rehearsals may explain why some people excel to world-class standards. Following research, Dr K Anders Ericsson, Professor of Psychology at Florida State University, concluded that it takes a minimum of 10,000 hours of practice to master any skill to the highest level. Examples of people who have done this include Microsoft co-founder Bill Gates, The Beatles and numerous other high achievers.

Not everyone agrees, though, with the 10,000-hour theory. Vanderbilt University researchers have argued that intellect or in-born talent, not brute-force practice, makes overachievers what they are.

Behavioural simulation

Behavioural simulation is a relatively new method for creating a rehearsal experience. Participants review a short, hypothetical, ethical issue situation. Each person has an assigned role within an imaginary organization and receives varying levels of information about the scenario. Participants must then interact with each other to develop recommended courses of action, short term, mid term, and long term.

Simulations try to re-create the complexities of what really happens in organizations. They also rehearse the realities of tackling difficult situations with incomplete information. Through the rehearsal experience participants become aware of the various ethical, legal and social dimensions of business decisions. The rehearsal develops participants' analytical skills at resolving ethical issues. They come face-to-face with the complexities of ethical decision making in an organization.

There is research evidence that simulations bring home to people the importance of ethics, helping them understand and master how to manage conflicts.[5]

Virtual worlds

Virtual worlds are electronic versions of behavioural simulations. The environments exist only in cyberspace, like Second Life. They offer visually stimulating ways to explore social interactions of all kinds, including ethical dilemmas. This 'immersive' technology takes rehearsal to a new level of reality, adding more realism and further engaging individuals. Also, using avatars, with voice and text chat, people can try out scenarios of an ill-structured problem, such as an ethical dilemma. For example, researchers at Iowa State University and West Chester University of Pennsylvania are creating a virtual world where science and engineering students confront ethical issues in an engaging and safe environment.[6]

Virtual worlds mimic actual complex physical spaces. People interact with each other and with virtual objects and animated characters. They can elicit widely different responses that would be difficult or impossible to achieve by other means.[7]

Role play, virtual worlds and experiential learning or other dramatic means for creating rehearsal conditions are only effective when they stimulate human interactions and produce a sustained learning result. For example, an ethical rehearsal should:[8]

1 Help employees examine their own and other's responses to ethical choices posed by real-world cases, and fully engage their interest and attention.

2 Show why it's important to look beyond 'the rules' to identify and frame ethical issues – subjecting them to detailed examination and questioning.

3 Steer employees to consider their obligations to other stakeholders and to ask questions such as 'Who are my stakeholders?', 'How will my decision affect them?' and 'What will my stakeholders expect of me?'

4 Use dramatic examples and analogies to impress on employees that ethical principles apply just as much to business situations as to any other aspect of life where actions could harm others.

5 Make employees realize that ethical dilemmas are a fact of life; when occurring at work, the stakes can be high for both the individual and others; through rehearsals employees realize the importance of paying attention to the facts, relying on their imagination to consider options and consequences, and using their natural skills of logical analysis.

6 Enable employees to recognize ethical issues when they arise, what psychological and organizational factors prevent such recognition and how to counter them.

If the rehearsal you create in your company meets these kinds of criteria, it is likely to provide a visceral experience – something people 'feel' in their body, not just their mind. It can leave people inspired, energized and newly confident about trying new forms of behaviour. While using their normal logical thinking ability, the experience taps into their feelings or intuition, combining these with eventual action. The right form of rehearsal creates opportunities for people to use all of themselves, to shift fairly painlessly from one sort of behaviour to another.

Alcatel-Lucent

Alcatel-Lucent, an innovator in networking and communications technology, focuses its efforts to generate an ethical culture mainly on middle management. There is extensive, targeted training to help them be effective compliance role models and ethical leaders.

In 2011, the company developed a web-based ethical leadership training module aimed at more than 10,000 people globally. An extensive communication plan informed people managers of their role in continuing to enhance a culture of business ethics and integrity.

The company delivers formal anti-corruption training over the web and through in-person sessions. In 2010, it reached more than 29,000 employees globally, including corporate executives and employees who interact with external parties. The overall participation rate was 97 per cent and by the following year had achieved additional follow-up with 100 per cent completion across the target audience. The company meticulously follows through to see that everyone completes the learning experience.

The company's web-based ethics and integrity overview training is mandatory for all employees and contractors and includes an entire section on anti-corruption. Training courses are updated annually to ensure that they reflect current business needs and evolving regulatory requirements. All training is documented through a Compliance training roadmap and tracked to verify full participation through a Compliance dashboard.

In 2011, Alcatel-Lucent targeted key stakeholders with a comprehensive global ethics and compliance training programme of 12 specialized compliance courses. Topics included export compliance, preventing harassment and discrimination, privacy and data protection, ethics and integrity training, information security training for contractors and, most importantly, anti-corruption training.

The education and training is designed both to educate employees about their personal and professional responsibilities under the code of conduct and to instil an ethical culture that fosters a commitment to the highest levels of ethical business conduct.

Newmont

The Newmont Mining Corporation is one of the world's largest gold-mining companies, based in Denver, Colorado. It has nine sites around the world, including the United States, Ghana, Peru, Indonesia, Australia and New Zealand. Over a hundred years old, Newmont promotes its values and ethics through numerous awareness programmes, including 'Ethics Day' and a 'Got Ethics' promotion. An awareness campaign called 'Ethics Begins With Me' includes a manager's toolkit prompting small-team discussion about ethical behaviour.

During 2012, a 'Tell Your Story' campaign culminated in a contest for the most moving story in the autumn of 2012. Through this programme, stories of ethical behaviour and lessons relating to the topic were gathered from leaders and employees. These stories were shared throughout the organization in many venues and formats, including videos, town hall meetings, posters, training sessions and small-group discussions.

Action planning and action learning

A typical way of creating an effective rehearsal situation is to ask an individual employee or an entire team to develop and implement an action plan for the next three to six months, based on what they have learned. This again is learning by doing.

An action plan for senior employees may stem from reviewing a part of the company's business ethics programme and deciding that it requires more sustained support. An example might be recognizing the need to provide extra training over the next few months on the issue of gifts and gratuities. Another might be the need to develop a new policy on wastewater disposal.

Another approach is to use real-life business dilemmas to develop people's sensitivities to issues of bribery, safety recall, or sexual harassment and subjecting them to detailed analysis. For example, the chosen issue might be explored in terms of:

- the common good – assumes that whatever advances the common good is ethical;

- fairness – treating everyone the same, unless there are morally relevant differences between them;

- human rights – assumes that what is right is not just advancing some goal, but whether people are fully informed about some decision that will affect them;

- useful impact (utilitarian) – assumes that what is right is taking action to produce the best balance of benefits over harm.

In many situations, employees need to develop moral courage, for instance to speak up or confront a colleague over some action. Rehearsals may include an open dialogue about the ethical principles at stake, case studies, role-modelling by real-life exemplars, and practice at using what has been learned. The ultimate aim is to build usable skills in moral decision making.

As with skinning cats, there are many ways to achieve the result of people practising their ethical skills in a realistic setting. KPMG, for example, strives to integrate ethics training through many 'touch-points'. These include orientation, company-wide meetings, technical training, employee letters, and publications, as well as its website. KPMG also finds that the best of these opportunities is through technical training, which covers 20–100 hours each year and allows ethical issues to be presented in the context of daily decision making.

'Hands-on' experience, where employees face actual or hypothetical ethical dilemmas, trains them in how the organization would like them to deal with potential problems. Lockheed Martin, for example, has developed a training game called 'Gray Matters' that includes dilemmas to be resolved in teams. Each team member offers his or her perspective, helping other team members understand the ramifications of a decision for co-workers and the organization.

Making rehearsals matter

- Identify key risk areas that employees will face.

- Measure capability before rehearsals begin; test knowledge or decision-making ability.

- Provide a rehearsal experience that 'feels real', perhaps using interactive settings.

- Build into the rehearsal experience awareness that wrongdoing will never be supported by the organization; confirm that employee performance evaluations will take their conduct in this area into consideration.

- Through the rehearsal experience, show employees that they are individually accountable for their behaviour.

- Demonstrate that employee conduct must align with organizational reputation and branding.

- Provide opportunity to discuss the experience and share learning experiences.

- Measure knowledge retention or test ethical decision making and compare results against pre-rehearsal results.

- Rehearsals and training are important ways to support the ethics programme. Successful ethics management, though, depends less on formal methods of learning than on what employees perceive as fair, responsible leadership at all levels, and a culture where all the important elements seem consistent and aligned.

When Siemens changed course and abandoned bribery as a normal way of doing business in certain countries, many people had to unlearn old habits and acquire new ones. This is why cultural shifts are so significant, and have been called transformative. However, it does not necessarily make it a particularly comfortable experience and it's the job of leaders to reduce people's anxiety by helping them feel psychologically safe.

Rehearsals of various kinds are a powerful way to normalize the new learning and make it permanently acceptable. They allow employees to get to grips with new values and to understand new concepts.

ACTION POINTERS

- Give really clear guidance when introducing new rules of behaviour.
- Walk the talk to encourage imitation and identification.
- Create realistic scenarios of ethical dilemmas, giving employees practice at working through the implications.
- Use experiential learning to promote a highly interactive approach to learning to handle ethical situations.
- Adopt simulations as a way of bringing home the importance of ethics.
- Make sure that ethical rehearsals meet the six basic essentials.
- Ensure that whatever rehearsal method is used, it creates a visceral experience, something people feel in their bodies, not just their minds.
- Offer 'hands-on experience' where employees face actual or hypothetical dilemmas and learn how the organization would like them to deal with them.

Notes

1   Katzev, R (2002) 'The Enlightenment effect', anecdote and evidence: essays linking social research and personal experience, Xlibris, Philadelphia

2   Lunday, J and Barry, M (2004) Connecting the dots between intentions, action and results: a comprehensive approach to ethical decision making, The Workplace, *Ivey Business Journal*, March/April

3   Tenbrunsel, A *et al* (2009) The ethical mirage, Harvard Business School, Working Paper 08-012

4   A proprietary interactive approach developed by Maynard Leigh Associates

5   Ferrell, OC, Fraedrich, J and Ferrell, L (2011) *Business Ethics: Ethical decision making and cases*, 8th edn, South-Western Cengage Learning, Mason, OH

6   SciEthics Interactive project to release free simulation (2012) Iowa State University, 25 October

7   See, for example, Cram, A *et al* (2010) Using virtual worlds to elicit differentiated responses to ethical dilemmas, Ascilite 2010, Sydney

8   See, for example, Radcliffe, D (2011) Adapted training ethical decision makers, Cornell HRT Review, September

11 Sustaining:
Support

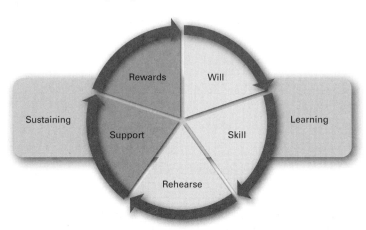

EXECUTIVE SUMMARY

- Constructing the support needed to underpin ethical behaviour in your organization is rather like completing a jigsaw.

- A successful shift towards a more ethical cultural can only be driven by senior leadership.

- Without addressing the root causes of unethical behaviour, your people may never come to realize the importance of acting ethically, nor will they feel fully supported in doing so.

- Difficult ethical issues can have a personal impact on employees that may not be immediately obvious to those who supervise or manage them.

- The organization needs to become clear about the precise aims of the support help on offer.

- A successful ethical culture cannot rely on enforced compliance of rules; instead, it builds awareness of the importance of using principles to guide ethical reasoning.

- Adequate support to individual employees must include raising each person's awareness of how to recognize ethical issues.

- When things are going well, people tend not to be particularly alert to ethical concerns.

- Effective support must aim to increase individual employees' certainty that they possess the skills and knowledge to find a solution to ethical issues.

The Hall of Fame is the world's largest jigsaw and consists of some 24,000 multi-coloured pieces.[1] No matter how good you are at jigsaws, it's likely to take you around six months to complete. Constructing the support to encourage ethical behaviour in your organization is rather like completing a jigsaw. There are lots of pieces available; fitting them together into a coherent picture can prove a lengthy challenge and there are few short cuts.

Throwing all 24,000 pieces of the Hall of Fame puzzle randomly onto the floor would be unlikely to produce a finished version. The right behaviour in an organization does not happen by chance either. Sheer diversity in large organizations can prevent agreement about what are ethical issues and what to do about them. In smaller enterprises, the scope for influencing ethical behaviours may be greater, yet the leadership will probably have less room to invest time and energy to effect change.

A successful shift towards a more ethical cultural culture can only be driven by senior leadership. The change requires both a strategic approach – setting up a formal ethics programme – and establishing support for ethical behaviour at the employee level. While senior managers tend to feel comfortable dealing with strategy, it's the employee, not the strategic, level that ultimately builds an ethical culture.

But why do employees actually need support for doing the right thing ethically? Surely ethical behaviour evolves naturally, from individual and interpersonal relationships? Won't it be enough just to employ people of character and integrity, and if necessary sensitize them to ethical issues? Unfortunately, like the Hall of Fame puzzle, it is not quite that simple.

Jigsaw enthusiasts soon learn to seek out certain key pieces, like those with straight edges or ones that clearly make up a corner. Likewise, in solving the right kind of support for ethical behaviour it may be sensible to start by looking at the root causes of unethical behaviour. Without addressing these, you may never complete the support jigsaw and your people may never come to realize the importance of acting ethically. Nor will they feel fully supported in doing so.

For example, if someone feels insecure in their job, speaking up about ethical concerns can seem unacceptably risky. What if colleagues resent their actions or the boss disapproves? Or if they do not believe the code of conduct is taken seriously by the company, why would they risk taking action about ethical issues encountered at work? (See Figure 11.1.)

Dealing with these root causes involves drawing support from diverse sources. Thankfully, there will be rather fewer pieces than the Hall of Fame puzzle, but like completing that monstrous jigsaw, it will take patience

FIGURE 11.1 Reasons why people act unethically: root causes of misconduct

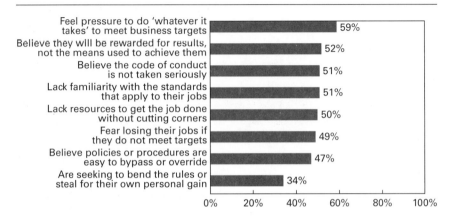

SOURCE: Forensic Integrity Survey: 2008–2009, KPMG LLP. With permission

plus constant trial and error. For example, suppose that your employees currently experience pressure to do whatever it takes to meet business goals. Then relevant support for ethical behaviour is likely to take the form of altering this destructive equation. The implications could be far-reaching. Managers and leaders may need to realign how they talk about goals, introducing the company's view that *how* you reach a goal matters as much as achieving the goal itself.

For example, at Gatwick Airport, which employs 2,500 people, the emphasis has been shifting away from the *what* to the *how* and as result, says HR Director Tina Oakley, 'We are getting really honest and targeted conversations in a way that was just not in this culture.'[2]

Difficult ethical issues can have a personal impact on employees that may not be immediately obvious to those who supervise or manage them. Someone facing a difficult choice between two conflicting 'right answers' may lose sleep, or worry about them during free time. For example, 'Shall I tell the supervisor my group is distorting the quality records?' Or 'Should I stay loyal to the group and say nothing?'

The response to such conflicts by many companies is to maintain ethics 'hotlines', providing out-of-hours support and the opportunity to ask questions or report concerns. The most effective ones function anonymously, throughout the year. Approximately half of all hotline calls occur at night or on the weekends. Alcatel-Lucent's Compliance Hotline, for instance, now operates in over 100 countries and handles well over 500 allegations annually. To promote transparency the company shares the resulting data across its 'compliance community'. The information allows it to monitor current issues and to encourage people to help improve the overall support programme.

Aims of support

In ensuring that the right ethical support exists at the individual level, the organization needs to become clear about the precise aims of the help on offer. Support to each individual should: raise awareness; increase knowledge; sharpen sensitivity; grow confidence; and build courage. Again, these cannot be 'ordered' from the top, but must be developed from below.

From the lofty confines of the executive suite, it might appear logical to devise a single, integrated form of assistance at the individual level. However, this is likely to be difficult and, given the diversity of the support elements, perhaps impossible. Different parts of the support system will have their own way of working. Many will use their own lines of command. Compliance staff, supervisors, trainers, those teaching codes of practice, supply chain managers and other stakeholders may all operate without continuous reference to either each other or any central 'support' mastermind.

Viewed from the outside, therefore, a wide-ranging support system for individual employees may simply look a disorganized mess. Or the reverse: to leaders it may appear misleadingly coherent, tucked neatly into the bureaucracy of the enterprise. Yet in reality, those on the receiving end may experience the result as disjointed, inconsistent or merely overwhelming. The way forward is to construct support around each individual employee. This does not imply a complex plan or vast resources. Rather it relies first on the tone set by leaders, who continually ask: 'What does the individual employee actually need?' Second, the answers will stem from a continuous, not one-off, dialogue, between each person and their immediate supervisor or line manager.

By building highly relevant ethical support around individuals, employees are more likely to start taking their ethical responsibilities seriously. For example, in a dialogue about ethical issues with a direct report, a supervisor can ask: 'Was the ethics training we gave you useful?' In contrast, the company's most senior leadership can only enquire strategically: 'Is the company's ethical training effective?' But the supervisor can discover the reality, and if the answer is negative, remedial steps can be set in motion.

Raise awareness

Rudolf Hoess, the man in charge of Auschwitz, believed that he was an upstanding German citizen, effectively doing his assigned job, and providing for his family in an honourable fashion. By following the orders of his superiors and performing his role, he believed that he was contributing to his own honour and the honour of a larger system. In Hoess's mind, he was an ethical person.

We like to think that Hoess was a monster, unlike any of us. Yet the man described is relatively ordinary, one whose evil actions were performed in the context of his professional life. Often, managers and other professionals justify their decisions by saying: 'I'm just doing my job. If we don't get that contract/sale/lower price, my career won't advance and my organization will be hurt.'[3]

It might seem obvious that we would immediately recognize an ethical situation, especially one involving evil actions. Yet psychological research shows that this is untrue. Often we completely miss the ethical aspect of a situation or feel that our 'superiors' must know what they are doing and should be obeyed, regardless of the implications for others.

A successful ethical culture does not rely on enforced compliance with rules. Instead, it builds awareness of the importance of using principles to guide ethical reasoning. Surveys suggest that most (79 per cent) employees agree that ethics are important in continuing to work for their employer. Yet around one in five employees are not concerned about the ethical environment of their organization. This group is complacent and their awareness levels will not increase without active guidance and ethical leadership. Without raising this awareness, there remains considerable potential for misconduct.

How?

Adequate support to individual employees must therefore include raising each person's awareness of how to recognize ethical issues. Ways to achieve this include:

- formal training, in which people learn the nature of ethical dilemmas and how they arise;
- discussions, preferably regularly using actual examples of live issues;
- actual practice – see Chapter 10, in which employees rehearse how they would tackle different ethical issues;

- circulation of regular news and information about other people's experiences of successfully facing ethical issues.

Sharpen sensitivity

Relevant support to the individual includes sharpening their insight into the implications of different actions through interpretation, analysis, evaluation and discussion. In particular, it should enable them to see:

- the nature of the situation and understand it, including the people and actions involved;
- possible ethical problems in a situation, and realize that those involved have rights and responsibilities;
- the likely outcomes of ethical choices and how the actions would affect specific people;
- what sort of people would be affected by those outcomes or consequences.

When things are going well, people tend not to be particularly alert to ethical concerns. Yet these are precisely the times when employees should be made aware of the dangers lurking in many situations. Adequate support therefore maintains the momentum, reminding employees that they should be watchful and ready to deal with dubious ethical situations.

How?

Sensitizing people to ethical dilemmas involves 'creating a movie in people's minds', giving them an actual experience that brings the issue to life, making it visceral, that is, felt in their body, not just their mind. This focuses not so much on ethical analysis as on implementation. It asks question such as: 'What if I were going to act on my values? What would I say and do? How could I be most effective?' It's a way of helping people voice their values and builds the muscle to do so.[4] Ways to create this include the following.

Theatre play

Employees use drama-based methods to become engaged with, and resolve, ethical dilemmas:

- Role play: improvised by employees who take on the part of a 'real' person and therefore try to experience how the choices may affect them, not merely logically but emotionally too.

- Forum theatre: uses actors to bring an ethical scenario to life, with employees commenting on the action and suggesting what the actors should do in each situation. So, for example, the employees might suggest what the protagonists should do to gain support for their actions; and whether they should refer the issue to another person – such as a supervisor or a compliance department; and whom they should inform about the issue – such as a team leader, line manager or an independent helpline.

Storytelling

Employees hear real stories about ethical dilemmas faced by colleagues elsewhere in the organization and learn how they tackled them. Discussion might revolve around:

'Put yourself in that person's shoes.'

'What would you do and why?'

'Is this an ethical dilemma and why?'

'What are the risks of proceeding with the proposed action?'

'Who might be harmed by the proposed action?'

Actual encounters

This is another version of storytelling, except that employees meet actual people who have faced moral dilemmas in the business. They get to question them about what they experienced and how they dealt with it. The encounters might be with senior managers who share their reasoning for the decisions they took and explain the pressures that the situation created for them.

Scenarios

Examples of ethics simulations might involve scenarios about the misappropriation of company funds, personal values related to improper workplace relationships and the organization's compliance with regulatory controls.

Scenarios are a way of communicating an organization's ethical values, standards of behaviour and approach to speaking up about misconduct. Most of all they are stories, and as stories they engage and inspire people. As Tim Schultz, Director of Business Ethics and Compliance at Raytheon, puts it: 'A lot of training is "death by PowerPoint"; you have a different training experience when you watch a scenario. When you can visualize a situation, you will remember that before you're going to remember 30 slides.' Sandra Franklin, Compliance Officer at Stryker, says: 'Using case studies based on the industry of the trainees has real meaning – it reflects what they do on a day-to-day basis. A case study is never really relevant until it comes into your own territory.'[5]

Grow confidence

It usually requires more than just a hotline to build employees' confidence and motivation to speak up about malpractices. Nor will hotlines necessarily reduce worries about the consequences of highlighting unethical actions. Research into ethics-related actions shows that nearly all employees regard the support given to them by their direct supervisor and colleagues is of critical importance in building the ethical culture. For example, most employees (93 per cent) identify supervisor support for standards of ethical behaviour as essential, and the majority (94 per cent) also feel that co-workers' support is vital.[6] Making sure that supervisors can respond positively to employee queries therefore forms another part of the support jigsaw.

When people see their colleagues paying attention to ethics in the work-place, it helps them face reality, both good and bad – in the organization and themselves. Consequently, they start to feel more assured, can admit to facing difficult choices, and be more resilient in dealing with whatever comes their way. With confidence, they may start commenting and reporting on ethical issues, where before they might have stayed silent. This is why launching an ethics management programme may initially increase the number of issues to be dealt with, because people are now more willing to come forward.

Effective support will therefore aim to increase individual employees' certainty that they possess the skills and knowledge to find a solution to ethical situations.

How?

Once people have practised using ethical tools (see Chapter 10), they are ready for less intense support that can help sustain them in their work situation. This might include:

- Regular meetings to share recent mutual experiences.
- Regularly inviting employees to comment on an ethical decision in three ways: is it legal, is it right, and is it beneficial? Share the results between all those involved.

- Reminders about what it means to be ethical, to take responsibility, to act as a role model.
- Inviting certain employees to become ethical champions.
- Celebrating exceptional ethical decision making in a public arena.

Apart from values, we all have a personal narrative or story about ourselves that can help us face ethical choices. Getting in touch with that story, articulating it aloud and sharing it with others, can build confidence.

Build courage

Cynthia Cooper changed corporate America. Once Vice President of Internal Audit at the now notorious WorldCom, she chose to investigate anomalies in the company's accounting entries and ended by inspiring major new legislation. Being a whistleblower at her level was certainly a personal challenge: 'It's important to be able to dig down and find your courage, which isn't always so easy. My mother would say, don't ever allow yourself to be intimidated. That was really ingrained in me, and I think that helped.'[7]

Cooper's experience is echoed in the comments of the Institute of Chartered Accountants of Scotland in introducing a review of ethical dilemmas: 'It is essential that professional accountants and others in business are able to display ethical courage.'[8]

But it is one thing to belong to a well-organized profession such as accountancy and show courage in highlighting bad practices. It is quite another to be an ordinary frontline employee who must make difficult ethical choices. The fate of most whistleblowers, for example, hardly encourages much personal bravery here.

Knowing what information or help employees need to make better ethical decisions is not just down to common sense. Often people must choose between right and right, or even between wrong and wrong. A myriad of individual and situational factors influence employees' decisions to behave ethically or unethically: researchers have identified background, personality, decision history, managerial philosophy, and reinforcement as important factors determining employees' behaviour when faced with ethical dilemmas. Therefore, useful support is not telling people that they must analyse a situation, though that can be a stimulus; helpful support will develop people to voice their values and therefore to:

- accept responsibility for confronting ethical issues;
- be willing to seek help and readiness to report on matters of concern;

- handle conflict and the risk of unpopularity or colleagues' disapproval;
- speak up for the organization's core values.

Where does such courage come from? How do individual employees marshal their own resources and bravery to act ethically? It cannot happen by the top team issuing a directive, or by a head of a department or business unit instructing his or her people to be courageous ethically.

Faced with difficult choices, people may have self-doubt, feel timid about standing up to bosses or be worried about the reaction of colleagues. Building employee courage comes through a combination of knowledge, confidence and space to reflect on one's own values and to voice personal values, expressing concerns and fears while knowing that the supervisor or line manager will readily and sympathetically explore these issues with you.

How?

Courage means the ability to face down imaginary fears and take the power to do what needs to be done, despite potential obstacles. Research from the Second World War and people who risked their lives helping others suggests that thinking about ethical issues long before you confront them gives people a head start in courage.

To support employees in building their courage to act in an ethical way:

- Ask employees to share examples of courage in dealing with ethical dilemmas.
- Use consciousness-raising sessions about personal values and relate these to corporate values.
- Supply facts about how the company supports courageous actions.
- Create awareness that unless you take risks you make no progress.
- Develop awareness of what it means to be accountable for ethical performance.
- Create learning experiences in which intuition plays an important part in making choices.
- Ensure supervisors and managers systematically encourage employees to seek feedback about ethical choices they face.
- Provide practice at giving constructive feedback.
- Encourage people to share their life stories and what really matters to them.

The last of these actions is based on the assumption that people actually know what to do and just have to figure out how to make it happen.

Conclusion

Finally, there is no one right way to create a fail-safe support effort. As we have seen, your company's support to employees is likely to be rather like a jigsaw, consisting of many pieces that together make up the total picture.

Based on actual experience, it probably does not matter if there is no tight central control over defining and managing all the elements, so long as the broad strategy prompts relevant support at the individual level.

ACTION POINTERS

- Give priority to building support at the employee level, rather than trying to create a company-wide, entirely comprehensive, strategic approach.

- Review the root causes of unethical behaviour as pointers for what kind of support to arrange.

- Introduce to your direct reports and colleagues the idea that 'how we reach a goal matters as much as achieving the goal itself'.

- Become clear on the precise aims of the support on offer to employees.

- Promote a continuous, not one-off, dialogue about ethical issues between each person and their immediate supervisor or line manager.

- Build awareness among employees of the importance of using principles to guide ethical reasoning.

- Avoid placing too much reliance on a hotline service to encourage people to speak up about ethical issues.

- Focus attention on the quality of the interactions between employees and their supervisor or line managers in respect of support.

- Make sure that supervisors can respond positively to employees' queries about ethical matters.

- Build employee courage by ensuring that they acquire knowledge, have the opportunity to reflect on values and to voice their concerns and fears.

Notes

1 See, for example, http://www.worldslargestpuzzle.com/hof2.html

2 Clegg, A (2012) Interview with Tina Oakley, HR Director at Gatwick Airport, *People Management*, August

3 Swenson Lepper, T (1996) Ethical sensitivity, cognitive mapping, and organizational communication, University of Minnesota, Minneapolis, *Electronic Journal of Communication*, 6 (4)

4 See, for example, the experiential learning approach pioneered in the UK by Maynard Leigh Associates using ideas drawn from the performing arts (www.maynardleigh.co.uk), and also Gentile, MC (2009) Giving voice to values, Aspen Institute: http://caseplace.org/d.asp?d=3142

5 Bradshaw, K (2012) Use scenarios and bring your code of ethics to life, Ethical Corporation, 30 November

6 Based on average of various international studies.

7 Ripley, A (2008) Q&A: Whistle-blower Cynthia Cooper, *Time*, 4 February

8 ICAS (2009) Shades of grey: ethical dilemma, Institute of Chartered Accountants of Scotland, Edinburgh

12 **Sustaining:** Rewards

EXECUTIVE SUMMARY

- What you measure, reward and discipline signals your leadership priorities.

- Ethics officers and their bosses often do not realize that they must underpin ethics programmes with appropriate incentives.

- Organizations and their stakeholders don't behave ethically by chance.

- Excessive reliance on extrinsic rewards may not motivate people to 'do the right thing.'

- The reward strategy should encourage quality decisions, not the achievement of goals.

- Rewarding the right behaviour should become part of the company's DNA.

- Gearing executive pay to the pursuit of ethical business practices is likely to be a growing trend, at least in developed economies.

- There is often insufficient or even no link, between behaving ethically and how the company measures personal performance.

- Communication of the reward strategy should create a buzz in the company.

- Continuous ethical improvement is the mark of a healthy ethical climate and shows that the reward system is working.

Napoleon famously said that he could find nobody willing to die for money but found legions of people who would be honoured to die for a ribbon. The first employer to recognize the power of rewards to shape human behaviour was Cyrus the Great, founder of the Achaemenid Empire, modern-day Iran. To encourage construction workers to rebuild the Jerusalem Temple in 538 BC, he held ceremonies consisting of a shoulder pat, a beverage, and a coin featuring his head.

Coming rather more up to date, in a mass mail to everyone in Barclays, newly appointed CEO Antony Jenkins wrote in 2012 about a radical change in the bank's reward system. 'How we do business, our impact as a company and adherence to our values will be considered as important as financial targets when assessing performance.'[1]

What your organization chooses to measure, reward and discipline sends signals about your leadership priorities. These can have a profound cultural effect, particularly if you choose to use people's promotion, pay and careers to reward ethical behaviour. Most organizational incentive systems are designed to produce financial results. Similarly, organizations rely heavily on using economic tools and models to steer the ship. It is as if 'making the numbers work' can always get the company to its destination. These are seldom directed towards influencing ethical behaviour.

We are used to incentives in business, homes, schools and other contexts. However, using them in compliance and ethics programmes has been slow to catch on. This is partly because many of those concerned with ethics do not realize that they must underpin their programmes with appropriate incentives. Consequently, the idea of deliberately creating a rewards strategy may be alien, even to those companies taking seriously the pursuit of an ethical business.

Investing time and resources in planning for marketing, product placement and purchasing is second nature to most organizations. The equivalent effort focused on ethics and motivating people's ethical behaviour is usually absent. Yet designing effective rewards that encourage individual ethical behaviour needs a similar thoroughness. You are unlikely to achieve a sustained cultural impact by relying on a random or unorganized effort.

Organizations and their stakeholders don't behave ethically by chance. Achieving correct ethical performance cannot sensibly be left solely to the influence of external regulation. Some companies, though, have given up entirely on deciding what's ethical. Instead, they rely on what's legal as their standard for decision making generally. The result is moral bankruptcy. 'We're not accusing you of being illegal, we're accusing you of being immoral', said Parliamentary Public Accounts Committee Chairman Margaret

Hodge to executives of Google, Amazon and Starbucks at the end of the hearings about these companies' apparent failure to pay their fair share of UK taxes.

No matter how much legal and compliance oversight exists, these cannot fully affect what happens behind company doors. When Kevin Rollins, President of the Dell Computer Corporation, was asked about the role of ethics in business, he paraphrased Russian dissident Aleksandr Solzhenitsyn: 'I've lived my life in a society where there was no rule of law. And that's a terrible existence. But a society where the rule of law is the only standard of ethical behaviour is equally bad.'[2]

Ethical behaviour in business needs to be deliberately created, much like the effort to achieve profits, shareholder value, return on investment, or any other desired performance outcome. To generate it, you have the initial choice of relying on two basic kinds of rewards: *extrinsic* – tangible or 'transactional', for work undertaken in employment, eg salaries, pensions, overtime; and *intrinsic* – from work and employment, eg engagement, creativity, job satisfaction, sense of teamwork, feeling valued.

These represent an important distinction between how leaders and managers can go about steering people's ethical behaviour. For example, too much reliance on extrinsic rewards may fail to tap into people's motivation to 'do the right thing'. Managers tend to have a strong bias in favour of extrinsic incentives. They rely too heavily on financial rewards, underestimating the importance of intrinsic motivation.

Leaders and managers therefore have potentially many ways to influence ethical behaviour in a company. (See box 'The rewards menu'.)

The rewards menu

Compensation: pay for services rendered; fixed and variable pay; short-term incentive pay; long-term incentive pay.

Benefits: supplement to cash compensation; social insurance; group insurance; pay for time not worked, access to facilities etc.

Work–life: active support to help employees achieve success at both work and home, such as work flexibility, paid time off etc.

Performance and recognition: acknowledgement or giving special attention to employee actions, efforts, behaviour or performance.

Development and career opportunities: learning experiences to enhance employees' applied skills and competencies; plans for an employee to advance their career goals.

Given the wide variety of rewards, leaders and managers must help individual employees understand why ethical performance can satisfy their self-interest and goals. Insightful managers shape employees' ideas about self-interest by devising incentives that reward cooperation and reinforce the pleasure that people take in collaborating with each other.

Some organizational cultures, though, dislike the idea of offering incentives for ethical behaviour. There may be a sense that it's wrong to reward people for doing what they should be doing anyway. For example, in the short term it makes little sense to pay staff extra for *not* fiddling their expenses! Where people feel part of a group, rewarding one individual for some ethical action may be resented, cause disharmony and make the person uncomfortable. Where this action involves informing management of an ethical issue, the person's colleagues may feel betrayed or let down in some way.

In building the rewards strategy, a further choice is between the carrot and stick approach. Both can shape human behaviour, but generally managers and supervisors shy away from using punishment, preferring to avoid conflict or to maintain good relations with staff. Yet punishment for acting unethically makes perfect sense in some situations.

People learn from observing the rewards and punishments of others. They don't have to experience these themselves in order to draw conclusions about how best to behave. For example, everyone watches and learns from what happens to those who do something unethical, such as bullying or sexually harassing colleagues. If the organization takes strong and early action, they will take their cue from this and feel less free to indulge in the same behaviour.

Spelling out the consequences for behaving unethically is as much a part of the reward strategy as offering benefits for doing the right thing:

> We expect every employee to uphold our ethical business practices. Each manager is responsible for the behaviour of those under his or her control or direction. Failure to comply with the standards in this statement will result in disciplinary action which may include termination of employment. We may also report the matter to the public authorities for appropriate action. (Cadbury Schweppes, 2008, Our Business Principles)

As you review your ethics programme for achieving the right forms of behaviour, you may well conclude, like many others have done, that it's better to reinforce correct performance through rewards, rather than concentrate on punishments. Since these can take many forms (see box on page 192), the ethics programme needs to evolve a suitable reward strategy:

- Be seen as fair by recipients and others in the organization.
- Be easy to explain and quickly understood.
- Be timely – following rapidly from desired performance.
- Give rewards that reflect the scale of the achievement.
- Deliver an element of surprise – it should not be taken for granted by the recipient.

Even if the reward strategy meets these criteria, its overall focus should be on encouraging high-quality decisions, rather than being goal driven. That is, the company is not just concerned with profits or sales, but *how people get there*, through, for example, integrity, teamwork and excellence. At Staples, for example, 40 per cent of every employee's performance appraisal is devoted to *how* an employee did his or her job.[3] An obsession with ends rather than means can lead to offering rewards that unexpectedly distort behaviour in the wrong direction. What looks like an initially good outcome may turn out to be an ethical and costly disaster.

It is therefore important to systematically analyse the implication of different sorts of rewards for good and bad ethical outcomes. By rewarding people mainly for achieving some kind of business goal, they are more likely to engage in unethical behaviour, such as cheating by overstating their performance. This is especially so when employees fall just short of their goals.[4]

Building the reward strategy

Unethical practices by organizations continue to generate a hunger for change. In many countries there is a popular desire for leaders who can be trusted and for businesses to act with integrity. Increasingly, the market, in the form of share prices, retaining stock, the ability to raise capital and the attraction and retention of talent, is driving alert firms to show publicly their strong commitment to corporate ethical behaviour.

Alongside these forces, local and supranational legislation is requiring companies to put ever-tighter ethical practices in place. Consequently, many firms find that it makes sense to establish formal ethics programmes supported by elaborate administrative systems such as risk assessment and compliance management. Together they are nudging business cultures to move in the right direction.

Professional risk managers, for example, are valuable both because they identify and quantify risk and bring the ethics programme alive. They can help move it from good intentions and the drawing board to ways that directly impinge on daily behaviour. Their expertise can steer senior management to devise reward strategies that encourage, rather than discourage, high ethical standards of conduct.

Devising this game plan is a critical piece of the ethical culture jigsaw. Without it, the support structure for ethical behaviour will remain incomplete.

Even in middle-sized companies, the ramifications of the reward strategy will be widespread. Upper management can therefore hardly avoid taking a close interest in deciding what the organization will reward and how this will reinforce stakeholders' ethical behaviour. The strategy will have many facets, including sanctions for engaging in, tolerating, or condoning improper conduct. Consequently, the best approach in devising the strategy is a holistic one, aiming to influence all aspects of employee life, and a series of overlapping triggers that precipitate change, rather than finite, rigid steps. The triggers are not 'owned' by a small core group, but may involve many people across the organization to make the reward strategy affect the entire culture (Figure 12.1).

Trigger 1: Identify

Begin by describing the actual ethical behaviours you want to embed in the culture. If the reward system works, people would behave in ways that you could actually see. So what observable behaviours would you expect to see throughout the company?

Using this first trigger, the corporate aim is to identify anything in how the organization works that might deter the desired behaviour from happening. Many people may need to contribute to producing a full picture of how the present culture might be getting in the way of people behaving ethically. Do these obstacles consist of people, systems or processes? How could the obstacles be removed or their impact reduced?

Trigger 2: Review

There is a large menu of formal and informal reward mechanisms for encouraging individual ethical behaviours. It includes ways for all employees to draw attention to excellent and less desirable workplace ethics. This might be through peer nominations, the actions of supervisors, independently

FIGURE 12.1 The reward strategy

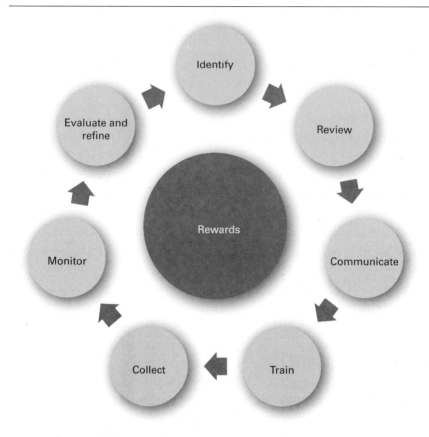

managed hotlines, an ombudsperson, an external agency offering support, suggestion schemes and contact with ethical champions.

In an ethical business, rewarding the right behaviour should become second nature, part of the company's DNA. For example, in 2008, Siemens became one of the first commercial enterprises anywhere to make compliance with the company's business rules for ethical behaviour part of its compensation system for top management. Others have since followed. The remuneration and incentive system says a lot about your company's culture and how seriously you take the issue of business ethics.

When leaders, managers and supervisors accept their normal responsibility to pursue ethical business practices, it makes constant reminders from senior management less necessary.

Whatever business you are in, there is growing recognition of the need to gear executive pay partly to the pursuit of ethical business practices. Never before has top-tier reward been so directly linked to brand and reputation. Attitudes have changed irrevocably as organizations become subject to strict accountability by the so-called 'shareholder spring', legislation, scrutiny of the media and wider public concern. The required response is not for sound-bites or paying lip service to good practice. It's about a deep and comprehensive strategy supporting culture change for ethical and responsible behaviour.

As part of this societal shift, there is likely to be continual and ever-strengthening demands for executive remuneration to be fair, equitable and about achievement, including ensuring ethical performance at both the individual and the corporate level.

But why do managers and supervisors *need* to be rewarded for promoting ethical business behaviour? Surely they are merely doing their job properly? But for most middle managers, being ethically mindful does not come naturally. They are mainly well-intentioned people who nevertheless often fail to consider moral issues when making decisions and taking action. They are prone to act without being values driven and without considering the ethics of business behaviour. This is why shifting the corporate culture is so important. The aim is to influence managers and supervisors to revise their expectations about both their own and other people's behaviour.

In refining your reward strategy you may wish to take into account the implications of recent research. This points the way to making better choices about how to encourage ethical behaviour. For example, a study of full-time employees by Deloitte in 2007 identified what promotes ethical workplace practices, namely: the behaviour of management, the behaviour of a direct supervisor, positive reinforcement for ethical behaviour, compensation such as salary and bonus, and the behaviour of peers. The analysis concluded that 'the behaviour of management (42%) and direct supervisors (36%) coupled with positive re-enforcement for ethical behaviour (30%) are ranked as top factors in promoting an ethical workplace'.[5]

Further confirming evidence about incentives to encourage ethical behaviour stems from the now annual rankings of the World's Most Ethical Companies. Just over half the best-performing firms encourage ethical behaviour using formal evaluation for promotion decisions (Figure 12.2).

Rewards therefore play a major role in shifting the critical mass of an organization towards being ethically minded. You may not see this happening in any obvious way but you can look for a most basic piece of evidence – would a new executive arriving in your company detect a clear link between behaving ethically and how the company measures personal performance? Senior leaders and their boards regularly fail to establish this

FIGURE 12.2   Incentives used to encourage ethical behaviour

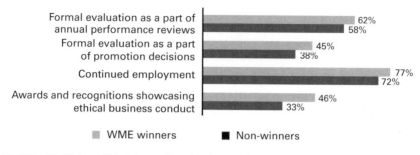

Formal evaluation as a part of annual performance reviews — WME winners 62%, Non-winners 58%

Formal evaluation as a part of promotion decisions — WME winners 45%, Non-winners 38%

Continued employment — WME winners 77%, Non-winners 72%

Awards and recognitions showcasing ethical business conduct — WME winners 46%, Non-winners 33%

■ WME winners   ■ Non-winners

SOURCE: World's Most Ethical Companies, Ethisphere. With permission

vital link. Instead, they take for granted issues like integrity, respect and trust, assuming that these will automatically occur. Yet this overlooks a simple rule: you increase the chances of desired behaviour happening by rewarding it.

The reverse is also possible. Badly chosen incentives can undermine ethical behaviour, or in extreme cases even encourage unethical actions. Could your reward system do that? For example, after a tough trading period in the early 1990s, the US company Sears Auto Center altered how it paid its mechanics. Their pay now depended on how many repair jobs they completed within a given period of time. Service advisers, who consulted with the mechanics about a vehicle's condition and then advised customers on potential repairs and parts, were put on a base salary plus commission plan. They also had to meet product-specific sales quotas.

It all went wrong. The auto-centers regularly overcharged customers for repairs. Worse, they recommended unnecessary work, even charging for repairs that hadn't been done. A government enquiry pinpointed the culprit as the commission-and-quota compensation system. It was an ethical, legal and reputational shambles that cost the company dear.[6]

Similarly, Green Giant, a unit of General Mills, once had a problem in one of its plants: packages of frozen peas kept turning up containing bits of insects. The cause was not a sudden infestation that had taken the factory by surprise. Hoping to improve product quality and cleanliness, managers had designed an incentive scheme in which employees received a bonus for finding occasional insect parts. Employees responded by bringing insect parts from home, planting them in frozen pea packages and then 'finding' them to earn the bonus. Incentives can enhance performance, but they don't guarantee that employees will earn them by following the most moral or ethical paths.

Research by Wharton management professor Maurice Schweitzer and colleagues demonstrates that when people are rewarded for goal achievement, they are more likely to engage in unethical behaviour, such as cheating by overstating their performance. This is especially likely when employees fall just short of their goals. Harvard Business School's Michael Jensen has gone so far as to propose that cheating to earn bonuses – such as by shipping unfinished products or cooking the books to exceed analysts' expectations – has become the norm at many companies.[7]

Reward desired behaviour to get more of it

- Celebrate examples of good ethical behaviour in your company newsletter.

- Award prizes for ethical behaviour: free dinners, small gifts, a day off; let the employee choose the reward.

- Declare an Ethics Day: allow every department to share their successes.

- Reward contrarians – people who disagree with or challenge the status quo. In its heyday, Motorola managers got ahead by challenging existing assumptions and by pointing out company weaknesses. In later decades the company lost those good habits.

- Promote people who consistently support company values and demonstrate ethical behaviour.

- Offer informal rewards: private praise, a special meeting with the chairman of the enterprise, a written thank-you note, or a verbal one in a social setting.

- Formal and informal rewards reinforce the enterprise's commitment to ethics.

Tesco gives 'Values Awards' to people it sees as doing the right thing, perhaps in exceptional circumstances. Only presented once or twice a year, these hard-to-obtain awards offer public praise and recognition. Often this is a simple postcard signed by a team leader or a director and presented in front of the person's peer group. Its rarity gives it a special importance. This kind of reward is based on the well-established finding that what most satisfies people is the feeling of improved self-worth from 'doing the right thing'.

Trigger 3: Communicate

All stakeholders and particularly employees need to know what's expected of them and the rewards the company uses to encourage their ethical behaviour. This is why leaders in search of an ethical culture often organize official presentations emphasizing the company's expectations. These can provide a high-profile launch pad for the reward system, by sharing the reasoning behind it and the nature of the sanctions systems.

At General Electric, Chief Executive Jeffrey Immelt demonstrates his concern for ethical leadership by beginning and ending each annual meeting with a statement of the company's integrity principles. He emphasizes: 'GE's business success is built on our reputation with all stakeholders for lawful and ethical behavior.' A reward system backs up his message by evaluating how well managers meet ethics-related standards. These may include ethics audits, minimal customer complaints and lawsuits, avoidance of compliance actions by government regulators, and high ratings on employee surveys.

Communicating the reward strategy should create a buzz: for example, by creating interest about the nature of the rewards, incentives and prizes employees will receive when they are nominated by their peers as well as their supervisors.

Ways to communicate about ethics are discussed in Chapter 7. In highlighting the rewards on offer, companies use ethics websites, monthly discussions, videos and team briefings. Another method is management by walking around, a technique introduced in the 1980s that many organizations still practise. Supervisors leave their office every day to talk with employees about ethical, as well as task, expectations.

Trigger 4: Train

While leaders and managers may grasp the purpose of the reward system, some may feel uncertain about choosing and applying the full range of rewards available. The reward strategy should therefore provide opportunities for all stakeholders to learn about the range of rewards and how to use them.

Executives and supervisors often benefit from help in developing their skills in talking about ethical behaviour and explaining the formal rewards on offer. Learning events can show them how to conduct public recognition sessions, or use informal awards to support ethical performance.

Informal awards tend to be more spontaneous and less tightly constructed than the formal ones. Consequently, training can help executives master the principles that govern the effectiveness of informal rewards. For example, they work best if they are highly individualized, spontaneous, immediate, symbolic, consistent, meaningful and simple.

Another learning aim is to develop awareness of the three easy ways to discover what employees would find rewarding:

- Watch what they do: how they spend their free time or what they might have as hobbies.

- Listen to them: discover their interests or workplace concerns, such as wanting more training.

- Ask them: use direct questions to throw light on motivations.

Training to use informal rewards

Learn how to determine the best way to deliver a particular reward, using:

- *If–then principle*: If an employee's ethical performance meets or exceeds your expectations, then reward the employee.

- *ASAP principle*: Give the reward as soon as possible after the performance has occurred.

- *Variety principle*: The reward should keep changing to retain its effect. The same reward given multiple times will lose its impact.

- *Sometimes principle*: Employees rewarded periodically when they perform well are likely to continue to perform well even without further awards.

See, for example, Informal rewards: what are they? Michigan State University, **http://www.hr.msu.edu/recognition/informalRewards.htm**

Trigger 5: Collect

Every time a manager encounters excellent ethical choices made by an employee, it's potentially another valuable story to share across the organization through the company's intranet, newsletters, team meetings and other gatherings. A strong corporate culture will generate many stories, myths and legends. Some will be inspiring, others perhaps amusing or memorable.

Within your reward strategy, allow for resources and time to collect such stories about actual ethical behaviour. Descriptions of ethical dilemmas and the decisions that people made about them can help others make sense of their own experiences and firm up expectations about ethical behaviour.

Incidentally, before making public a story of someone's ethical actions, check whether this person is happy to see their name up in lights. Not everyone will relish seeing themselves featured in the company's newsletter or highlighted on its intranet for doing what's right ethically. Sometimes it may be better to describe the situation and management's response without identifying individuals by name.

Trigger 6: Monitor

Underpin the strategy with a commitment to audit the use of rewards. This needs to happen at least once or twice a year. A regular check will reveal whether leaders, managers and supervisors are using the full range of rewards for shaping behaviour.

Regular monitoring can uncover difficulties that people may have in applying the rewards to actual situations; for example, do some rewards need to be refined or others dropped in favour of new ones? It should also confirm that when managers conduct employee appraisals, they include a review of ethics performance. That is, are managers and supervisors talking about ethical behaviour directly with each person in a formal setting? This is also a good time for making sure that the ethics code appears in all documents relating to employee evaluation.

Trigger 7: Evaluate and refine

The most difficult and important trigger is the process of evaluating the entire reward strategy. It's challenging because it is part of the wider task of assessing the entire ethics programme – how it's working and its effectiveness. This needs to take into account the basic tools that managers use to manage: goal setting, strategic, departmental and individual reward systems, performance appraisals and disciplinary practices. All of these will need to be evaluated not just against the broad corporate goals, but whether they serve to reinforce the ethics programme.

Even the most effective rewards strategy needs adjusting at some stage. Rather than allow it to continue unchanged, as if running on rails, it is sensible at least once a year to conduct a formal evaluation. This can help sharpen and refine the strategy to maximize its impact. Therefore, it is important not to allow this process to become entangled with the detail of individual rewards. Rather it should focus on the big picture:

- Is the present ethics reward approach working well enough?
- What is it costing us?
- Is it value for money?

Now is a time to involve all key stakeholders, including those who operate the rewards and those on the receiving end of them. Invite their help to judge the effectiveness of the overall reward system and explore fresh thinking. Although the process will be unique to your particular organization, it will probably deal with issues such as shown in the box 'Is it working?'

Is it working?

- Assess whether the existing reward strategy is achieving its agreed purpose. In most cases this will be 'to promote the existence of an ethical business in a cost-effective way'.

- Review the criteria for measuring the success of the reward process; are the measures still relevant?

- Relate the existing strategy to the organization's wider strategic objectives: for example, check how the strategy relates to other personnel strategies and plans.

- Ensure that the rewards strategy encourages compliance with legal requirements, codes of practice and organizational policy.

- Make new recommendations for the design and elements of the ethics reward structure.

- Review rewards in individual parts of the organization, and for a range of jobs at different levels: if necessary, adjust levels of reward for individuals and groups.

- Establish whether the rewards maximize the motivation and therefore the contribution and commitment of individuals; is the system fair?

- Benchmark rewards to identify good practice: compare present rewards used with what other organizations use to promote ethical behaviour.

- Identify ethical issues where conflicts of interest or dilemmas arise and whether there's a need to adjust rewards.

- Ensure that there continues to be an adequate link between people's ethical performance and their remuneration and career progression.

A successful ethics reward programme cannot be measured by the number of employees who certify that they have read the corporate code or attended training sessions. Ethics concerns the organization's basic culture and operating values. This is about the pride and satisfaction that employees find in their work, the attention to quality and service, the degree to which suppliers and customers are treated fairly and honestly – all of which impinge upon the organization's overall reputation and success. The reward strategy is not just about achieving compliance, it is there to shape behaviour that will contribute to the values.

The mark of a healthy ethical climate is continuous ethical improvements. Therefore the seventh trigger above is not a final one, nor is it a single 'step' that once taken ends the entire reward process. Rather it's a part of a continuous effort to develop and improve the reward strategy and its contribution to running an ethical business.

ACTION POINTERS

- Help individual employees understand why ethical performance can satisfy their self-interest and goals.
- Reinforce correct performance mainly through rewards, rather than relying on punishments.
- Consider the balance between extrinsic versus intrinsic rewards for ethical behaviour.
- The overall strategy should encourage high-quality decisions rather than being goal driven.
- Treat the creation of the rewards strategy as a series of at least seven discrete triggers.
- Describe the observable ethical behaviours that you want to embed in the culture.
- Identify what might stop people behaving ethically in your particular culture.
- Make sure that there is a recognizable link between pay and ethical performance.
- Make sure that the communication of the reward strategy creates a buzz in the company.
- Conduct a formal evaluation of the rewards strategy, at least annually.

Notes

1 Treanor, J (2012) Barclays 'will be about values, not just value', *Guardian*, 14 September

2 Maxwell, JC (2003) *There's No Such Thing as Business Ethics: There's only one rule for making decisions*, AOL Time Warner Book Group, New York

3 Treviño, L and Nelson, K (2011) *Managing Business Ethics: Straight talk about how to do it right*, 5th edn, John Wiley & Sons, Inc, Hoboken, NJ

4 The problem with financial incentives – and what to do about it (2011) Knowledge@Wharton, 30 March, http://knowledge.wharton.upenn.edu/article.cfm?articleid=2741

5 Leadership Counts: 'Deloitte & Touche USA 2007 Ethics & Workplace' survey (2007) Deloitte & Touche

6 See, for example, Mitchell C *et al* (2005) Rewarding ethical behaviour, *workspan* magazine, WorldatWork, July

7 See Note 4 above

PART FOUR
Sustaining the shift

Over the horizon: 13
The future of ethical leadership

EXECUTIVE SUMMARY

- Leaders unable to show a strong commitment to ethics will find it severely career limiting.

- Ethical guidance will be shaped by megatrends: globalization; society shifts (societal change); demographic shifts; technological advance; and the requirements for a low-carbon economy.

- Being unethical, or simply hypocritical about ethics – saying one thing but doing another – is becoming less easy in an era of ever-greater transparency.

- There is likely to be more emphasis on collaborative leadership and flattened hierarchies will have a stronger appeal, creating in turn new forms of ethical challenges.

- Global environmental problems create their own ethical complications and include the big three: climate change, resource depletion and toxic materials, and eco-efficiency.

- Sustainability and the search for low-carbon solutions will become increasingly urgent during the 21st century and will affect what it means to be an ethical leader.

- Tomorrow's ethical leader will be searching not just for profits but also for how to build relationships that release the combined energy and creativity of people inside and outside the organization.

- Future ethical leaders will need to understand the nature of engagement and its implications for how they lead.

- The new type of ethical leader will develop a much sharper instinct for respect – an awareness of the importance of honouring human rights and building workplaces that offer full inclusion.

- What is coming over the horizon demands a leader who views ethics as '*doing the right things that are not required to be done*'. This kind of person 'does right even though nobody is looking'.

'**A** map that tries to answer every question for every person is effectively unreadable', says Google's Head of Mapping, Brian McClendon.[1] The same applies to mapping ethical leadership. A comprehensive description of future ethical leadership is impossible, and would probably be useless for practical business purposes. The clearest landmark for knowing your way around ethical leadership territory will be, as now, *willingness to set the ethical tone for your company*.

Setting the tone emerges most strongly when confronting live ethical dilemmas. There is nothing academic or abstract about this activity. It involves real situations – ones requiring corporate leaders to step out from the shadows and establish what it means to be ethical. Retreating behind the security of laws and regulations will leave them and their company exposed to serious reputational damage, or worse.

Take, for example, the hoax phone call made during 2012 to the hospital where the UK's Duchess of Cambridge – a future queen of Britain – was undergoing treatment for severe morning sickness. Two Australian radio presenters managed to convince a nurse on duty that they were phoning from Buckingham Palace on behalf of the Queen. All good knock-about stuff, you might think. Surely that is what some radio stations do? It makes for good listening figures, in this case even headlines around the world. It certainly was not strictly illegal in either the UK or Australia.

Yet sadly, the nurse in question was found dead shortly afterwards. The hospital denied that she had been in any way disciplined for how she had dealt with the call. But this jokey, apparently light-hearted incident turned instantly from a piece of fun into a serious lapse of judgement – one ending in someone's death. Whether or not the nurse committed suicide was not even known when the media headlines turned nasty. The radio station's manager immediately announced that he was taking the two hoax callers off the air for the time being. Now put yourself in the mental shoes of that unfortunate radio station manager. Do you become an ethical leader and declare that the station will never again sanction hoax phone calls? Should you even have allowed hoax calls in the first place, and do you now feel really bad for allowing it to happen, given that it ended in someone's death?

For some corporate leaders the answer is clear. They want to run a company that is open and honest. Staff would be expected to avoid deception, or underhand attempts to mislead people, merely to create an entertaining broadcast. Yet, nearby may be a highly responsible media company whose tactics rely on misleading individuals into revealing their criminal behaviour. In that company the arguments for what is ethical appear to be entirely different.

Future ethical leaders therefore cannot 'map the territory' and be sure that they have covered every location. If they could, it would be unworkable. Instead, what will be demanded of every future ethical leader are the following:

(a) It is better to try to be ethical than not try at all.

(b) It's your responsibility to set the tone for your company – guiding people about acceptable and unacceptable behaviour.

(c) To lead, you must rely on your own character, integrity and personal values to help steer the organization's unique moral compass.

In the past, being an ethical leader was often seen as exceptional, even transformational – 'morally purposeful and elevating'.[2] In the future, though, ethical leaders are likely to occur more often. Few of those in charge of large organizations will survive in their roles if they bury ethics under a blanket of compliance rules. Similarly, few of those running smaller organizations will avoid the impact of competitors who assume that there are major gains from following responsible business practices.

Future leaders will find it severely career limiting if they cannot show a strong commitment to ethics. When the chairman and CEO of Siemens failed to tackle their organization's addiction to bribery as a way of winning business, they were summarily removed. That kind of action is likely to happen more frequently. Corporations will expect their leaders to demonstrate integrity and possess a strong ethical compass. They will do so because, first, it makes commercial sense and, second, because the communities in which they operate will increasingly demand evidence of socially responsible behaviour which earlier leaders may have managed to avoid.

Tomorrow's ethical leaders will continue being the company's most senior ethics officer. This will require them to be adept at promoting core values, ensuring a workable code of ethics, and promoting ethical learning throughout their organizations. Given the changes on the horizon, they will therefore face a different scale of challenges from those their predecessors faced.

For example, providing ethical guidance to a company will be shaped by predictable, yet formative megatrends. These include: globalization; society shifts (societal change); demographic shifts; technological advance; and the requirements for a low-carbon economy. While their impact on future ethical leadership remains currently out of focus, we already see the main outlines of how they will affect ethical leadership.

Globalization

In 2011, the US authorities charged five leading US accountancy firms and their Chinese branches with violating security laws. The firms were accused of refusing to produce paperwork concerning investigations into accounting fraud at nine Chinese organizations. Such an action would have been ir-relevant 50 years ago, since the amount of business done in China would have been miniscule. For the leaders of the accounting firms, the new ethical considerations proved to be both complex and difficult. They complained of having to face competing tensions which left them violating laws in both countries – in the United States for failing to share documents, and in China for sharing them.[3] We can expect this kind of ethical dilemma to grow as globalization continues its inexorable advance.

Issues such as 'What is ethical?', 'What do we do when local ethical norms are so different to our own?' and 'How do we recognize ethical dilemmas in our attenuated supply chain?' pose leaders with more than just food for thought. As the accountancy example above shows, they represent excruci-ating dilemmas that need to be identified and resolved.

Reputational risk, too, grows with globalization, placing added demands on ethical leaders to guard their company's good name jealously. Research in 2012 into over 600 European companies found that an overwhelming 95 per cent had become more concerned about multinational risk over the past five years.[4] The cost of clearing up after serious ethical lapses can be daunting.

For example, in 2012, HSBC was held accountable for stunning failures of oversight for permitting narcotics traffickers and others to launder millions of dollars through HSBC subsidiaries. In announcing a fine of $1.92bn, the largest settlement of its kind, US Assistant Attorney General Lanny Breuer commented: 'The record of dysfunction that prevailed at HSBC for many years was astonishing.' The bank's CEO claimed: 'We have been taking concrete steps to put right what went wrong and to participate actively with government authorities in bringing to light and addressing these matters.'[5] The 'concrete steps' were not cheap, and involved hiring expensive high-ranking additional personnel to make sure that no more such lapses occurred.

Implications

1 Globalization is leading to complex moral challenges that leaders cannot afford to ignore.

2 For ethical leaders, the way through the moral maze is to build bridges between employees and external stakeholders, focusing on moral values and fairness in decision making.

3 Ethical leaders need to be particularly alert to increased reputational threats from globalization.

Society shifts (societal changes)

Around the world, business leaders face an inexorable trend towards 'individual empowerment', with big implications for ethics, or what it means to run a responsible business. For example, detailed analysis of global trends reveals a growing middle class. This will become 'the most important social and economic sector in the vast majority of countries around the world', according to a US government assessment published in 2012. Apart from a surge in 'individual empowerment', it will mean improved education and health-care, and widespread use of communications technologies.[6]

These developments suggest that worldwide attitudes towards ethical issues such as bribery, corruption, intellectual property theft, industrial espionage, and what is perceived as responsible business practices may well alter as a consequence. Though hard to fully understand at this stage, the likely changes will include renewed questioning of the value of never-ending growth, new demands for what many people want from work, greater accountability for business actions, more recognition of the power of engagement or lack of it, respect for fairness and how people are treated at work.

For example, the younger generation is highlighting the impending 'death of deference' in organizations. Most people are not looking for a job but for a company that they can have a relationship with. They don't just want a job, they want some meaning.

These and other shifts are already affecting ethical leadership, pointing to new leadership skills required for the 21st century. Quite simply, what it means to be an ethical leader is already altering. More than ever, it means accepting change, anticipating it and capitalizing on it.

In such a fluid landscape, organizations must adjust corporate cultures if the company is to be best placed to succeed. The leader's ability to make sense of the varied expectations of society will therefore be a continuing challenge, especially for those aspiring to run responsible companies.

For example, for leaders of global companies, society's expectation that a company will pay its 'fair share of taxes' has already surfaced as an important new ethical consideration: first, because tax systems will need adjusting in the face of global arrangements, and second, because *how* a company operates in society matters as much as what it does.

The future is already here for some companies, as when Starbucks offered to pay £20m in extra taxes when technically it was not required to do so. Here we see the power of social disapproval at work. Starbucks' leaders faced the ethical dilemma of being accused of not paying taxes, while shareholders took it to task for paying taxes unnecessarily.

In the past, business leaders might have got away with being unethical, or simply hypocritical about ethics – saying one thing but doing another. This is becoming less easy in an era of ever-greater transparency. Even being an ethically neutral leader – someone who lacks ethical awareness and cares mostly about himself or herself and the organization's bottom line, rather than other people – may prove to be hard to maintain.

Implications

1 Recognize that there are social pressures building up to run a socially responsible business and respond accordingly.

2 Assume that you will face ever-increasing transparency of data and shift the organization to work with this trend, rather than trying to subvert or prevent it.

Demographic shifts

The external environment of companies is complex, made more so by shifting demographics. The global economy is in flux, and the call for visionary, ethical leaders is unmistakable. For example, demographic changes are 're-shaping financial services, introducing additional demands on leadership at all levels'.[7]

Future organizations will need to prioritize the search for leaders who can help address the many challenges thrown up by important demographic movements. Ageing, ethnicity and gender, for example, seem destined to transform workplace arrangements dramatically. A democratic society that values excellence in performance and values individual human dignity will also develop ethics based on respect, competence and accountability. Ethical leaders are likely to find that they need greater awareness of how to introduce increased tolerance of differences and understanding of others.

Many of the ethical repercussions from demographic changes still remain hidden, or so far have had a relatively low profile as far as organizations are concerned. What, for instance, are the ethical implications for managing succession planning; changing work–life expectations, or the increased need for virtual and real-time communication? Demographic shifts will also help to redefine participation – old ways of leading may soon look obsolete. For example, in future, a collaborative style of leadership and flattened hierarchies will have a stronger appeal. In turn, these will create new forms of ethical challenges.

Many organizations have embraced the increased availability of older employees; others still fondly believe that they will be able to recruit younger age groups despite the demographics that suggest otherwise. With older employees likely to play a bigger part in company performance, in the future how they are treated and respected will matter far more than in the past. Similarly, the acceptability or otherwise of enforced retirement to make way for younger workers previously posed few problems for ethically minded leaders. This is set to alter as the demographic changes become more pronounced.

Implications

1 To make sense of demographic changes, ethical leaders should consider the impact that these shifts are already making in each area of the firm's activities, to avoid causing harm from company decisions and policies.

2 Ethical leaders are best placed to take the lead in pursuing needed developments in increased employee participation.

3 Be willing to rethink the hierarchy and whether it is likely to help or hinder the organization's ability to cope with ethical issues arising from demographic shifts.

Technological advance

The digital world continues to transform what it means to be human, and to live and work in society. Ethical leaders in the 21st century will therefore need to keep their wits about them in order to steer their companies through the moral maze. For example, in the world of cheap and almost limitless processing and storage capacity, there are huge, almost irresistible pressures from commercial and political interests to escalate the use of the electronic footprints we leave many times a day. The benefits of using personal information are undeniable. Yet so are the risks for individuals and society where use goes beyond reasonable expectations or where things go wrong.

The potential creation of comprehensive and highly centralized databases poses major ethical risks which tomorrow's leaders must confront: '... we have seen far too many careless and inexcusable breaches of people's personal information', claimed Richard Thomas, the UK Information Commissioner launching one of his regular annual reports. 'The roll call of banks, retailers, government departments, public bodies and other organizations which have admitted serious security lapses is frankly horrifying.' His agency had found Alliance & Leicester, Barclays Bank, Clydesdale Bank, Co-operative Bank, HBOS, HFC Bank, Nationwide Building Society, NatWest, Royal Bank of Scotland, Scarborough Building Society, The Post Office and United National Bank all in breach of the Data Protection Act and ordered them to sign formal undertakings.[8]

Elsewhere, continued developments of new applications of technology will cause ethical leaders to face new risks and concerns. For example, Cisco's global CEO has called advanced forms of collaboration via the web 'the biggest shift the company will have to make' in the next five years. It heralds moves from autocratic leadership towards collaborative decision making, from functions and silos to cross-departmental, global teamworking. All this will pose their own ethical challenges, some known, but many as yet unknown.[9]

Changes in technology include the development of neuro-enhancing drugs, already in circulation but likely to increase dramatically in the coming years.

These could be used to improve performance of those who do routine cognitive tasks – adjusting people to cope with unpleasant work, rather than trying to ameliorate the conditions of work. Employers could become abusive and coerce people into taking these new forms of enhancements.

Further into the future, yet already on the horizon, are dilemmas about whether to invest in potentially profitable innovations that imply controversial technologies. These include genetic manipulation or cloning techniques, potentially dangerous nanotechnologies or powerful artificial intelligence systems. These, too, seem destined to create serious ethical challenges for business leaders.

Implications

1 To ensure your own success as well as your organization's, you will need strong motivation to ensure that no harm comes to anyone as a result of the application of technology by your respective company. For example, Facebook's founders and leaders have the attention of half a billion people. Are they ready to demonstrate ethical leadership and operate with integrity, vision and not abuse their market dominance? Or, as one observer puts it: 'Will they succumb to the traditional business leadership paradigm and focus solely on financial outcomes?'[10]

Requirements for a low-carbon economy

Moving to a low-carbon economy is expected to make the next few decades different from anything we've experienced before. Global environmental problems create their own ethical complications and include the big three: climate change, resource depletion and toxic materials, and eco-efficiency. In the face of such complexity, ethically minded leaders may rightly wonder: 'How will these changes affect my organization?' 'How can I turn potential threats into opportunities?' 'What will a low-carbon economy actually look like?'

The answers have yet to emerge, but future ethical leadership will probably involve balancing the business case for action against the opportunities, threats of inaction, risks of action and the ethical dimension.

Sustainability and the search for low-carbon solutions will become increasingly urgent during the 21st century; this will affect what it means to be an ethical leader. This contrasts with the experience of previous generations of managers and leaders. In their race for 'progress', they often overlooked or ignored the broader needs of humanity. Sustainability is a relatively new business model producing a new ethic and today's leaders are only starting to get to grips with it. Future ethical leaders will need a passion, a vision, and considerable persistence. This will involve systems thinking with a long-time horizon and a willingness to keep learning – seeing the big picture and recognizing that organizations are highly interdependent.

Based on what we know already of the changes ahead, tomorrow's ethical leader will be searching not just for profits. He or she will also be building relationships that release the combined energy and creativity of people inside and outside the organization to make a difference. This will almost certainly involve a shift in corporate social responsibility. Long reduced to the unthreatening acronym CSR, this has its own ethic and its own unique implications for the future ethical leader. Take, for example, recycling. In Amsterdam, 99 per cent of local waste, both household and industrial, is already used to provide heat and energy for the city's metro, tram and road lighting; a similar system is used in other cities. In the future, corporate leaders may find that it is now regarded as morally wrong to allow their company's waste to go to waste.

Implications

1 Be aware of your company's growing obligation to its local community.

2 Expect to face pressures to demonstrate concern for social and environmental performance.

3 Honour the company's ethical obligations to its numerous stakeholder groups.

4 Incorporating environmental awareness into strategic plans may well give companies an ethical advantage in coming years.

Over the horizon

'We are at a crossroad for capitalism and corporate citizenship', claims the Executive Director of the Boston College Center for Corporate Citizenship.[11] The regulatory failures and financial meltdown since 2008 have shown how essential it is for companies everywhere to develop ethical behaviour, led by leaders who set the right tone and bring about cultural change. What tomorrow's ethical leaders will require is still not entirely in focus. Yet we can peer far enough over the horizon to realize what is coming and what will be needed.

The most certain requirement is for a new type of ethical leader. First, leadership generally will tend to be more widely distributed, with all kinds of people taking temporary leadership to tackle important issues and later reverting to their previous roles. This kind of leadership will view ethics in a rather different light to most present leaders, who often confuse compliance with integrity. Compliance protects an organization from regulation and public criticism. But it has little impact on day-to-day operations. Integrity lies at the core of an organization's activities, influencing every decision and activity. Future ethical leaders will therefore pay more attention to goals and how these are achieved, and be less dependent on laws and regulations for ensuring compliant behaviour.

Second, tomorrow's ethical leaders will be hell-bent on winning employees' full engagement. Why? Because they realize that engagement is the most cost-effective way of ensuring high levels of performance, including a commitment to ethical behaviour. Engagement remains a fairly contentious term, with critics arguing that it is just another way of talking about employee involvement. Terminology aside, there is growing awareness of the close link between employee wholehearted commitment and company performance. Future ethical leaders will therefore need to understand the nature of engagement and its implications for how they lead. They will therefore push far beyond basic ethics to create business cultures where people's involvement in the organization depends on their feeling valued, involved, developed and inspired (VIDI).

Third, the new ethical leader will spend more time and be more adept at scanning the environment – looking outside the immediate group for information; recognizing performance gaps – for example, realizing where the organization is, against where it wants to be; promoting open communications – ethical dialogue about moral questions; and encouraging continuous ethical education – commitment to a never-ending process of learning about ethical issues. This is far removed from the old command-and-control style of leadership, still prevalent in far too many organizations.

Fourth, the new ethical leader will be far more adept at combating the shadow side of the organization. This will involve creating zero-tolerance policies and ensuring action to tackle incivility, aggression, sexual harassment, discrimination and other destructive actions.

Finally, the new type of ethical leader will develop their instinct for respect – an awareness of the importance of honouring human rights and building workplaces that offer full inclusion. This will run in parallel with being more open, accepting that there is often no 'right way' of doing things and being more aware of people's built-in biases and assumptions. Figure 13.1 suggests some of the requirements for the new type of ethical leader.

FIGURE 13.1   What future ethical business leaders will need

This shopping list of attributes may seem daunting. But then so are the challenges coming over the horizon. Nobody will fulfil all of them completely. They merely suggest what future organizations will look for, even if they can seldom recruit a paragon of virtue to demonstrate them all.

The new ethical leader will not be someone acting in the traditional way of duly doing the right things that are 'required to be done'. Instead, what is coming over the horizon demands a leader who is more flexible, someone who looks beyond current rules and regulations and asks what needs to be done, and what is the right ethical thing to do. This kind of leader will also '*do the right things that are not required to be done*'. This kind of person does right even though nobody is looking.

Both now and in the future, ethical leaders will need to be courageous people, often doing what's right despite the obstacles. In the worst-case scenario, the corporate leader may inadvertently become the ultimate whistleblower, confronting colleagues or even the entire organization over its unethical behaviour. For example, the president and CEO of Olympus, Michael Woodford, precipitated a crisis by triggering an independent investigation to reveal a $1.7bn fraud. Not only was something rotten at the heart of this once-proud company, it raised the even more fundamental question: was something rotten in the entire country?[12]

Summing up

Based on an overall assessment of the trends listed above, we can at least conclude some fundamentals about the future ethical leader. He or she is likely to be far more socially responsible than previous generations of business leaders. This will only partly occur through personal choice. Society, community and global pressures will also play a major role in this expected shift. In practice, to be more socially responsible will mean that the new ethical leader will be highly resilient, able to withstand integrity challenges.

The new ethical leader will also enthusiastically use engagement, rather than carrots and sticks, to win cultural change. This kind of leader will aim to be inspiring, putting humanity and meaning at the heart of the organization. Again, while this will often happen through following personal values, external drivers will also play their part in the change.

In the service of long-term health and value, such leaders will have the courage to do what is inconvenient, unpopular and even temporarily unprofitable. They will tend to view the world as interconnected, needing multidisciplinary solutions to address complex problems that arise every day. In short, they will be an ethical leader for the 21st century.

ACTION POINTERS

- Show your commitment to business ethics and personal integrity and develop a strong moral compass.
- Consider yourself the company's chief ethics officer and act accordingly.
- Stay alert to ethical issues constantly being raised by the five megatrends of globalization; society shifts (societal change); demographic shifts; technological advance; and the requirements for a low-carbon economy.

- If you are not doing so already, explore the implications of collaborative leadership and flattened hierarchies and their ethical implications for your company.
- Get clear on the difference between compliance and integrity.
- Pay more attention to goals and how these are achieved, and be less dependent on laws and regulations for ensuring compliant behaviour.
- Seek to win employees' full engagement, because engagement is the most cost-effective way of ensuring high levels of performance, including a commitment to ethical behaviour.
- Encourage continuous ethical education – a commitment to a never-ending process of learning about ethical issues.
- Try to be a leader who views ethics as '*doing the right things that are not required to be done*'; be the kind of person who '*does right even though nobody is looking*'.

Notes

1 Rusche, D (2012) Unchartered territory, *Guardian*, 8 December

2 Bennis, WG and Nanus, B (1985) *Leaders: The strategies for taking charge*, Harper & Row, New York

3 Scannel, K and Bond, S (2012) SEC charges China units of top audit firms in fraud enquiry, *Financial Times*, 4 December

4 Kendrick, A (2012) Emerging risks are bringing the world to the boardroom door, ACE European Risk Briefing, December

5 McCoy, K (2012) HSBC will pay $1.9 billion for money laundering, *USA Today*, 11 December

6 Global Trends 2030, National Intelligence Council

7 Coping with complexity (2010) Deloitte

8 Rogerson, S (2007) Centre for Computing and Social Responsibility, and from ETHIcol in the *IMIS Journal*, **17** (4), August

9 Smedley, T (2011) Help leaders to drive change, *People Management*, April

10 Bradley Burns, A (2012) When will you grow up, Facebook? Huffington Post Tech, 22 May

11 Googins, B, Executive Director of the Boston College Center for Corporate Citizenship, in Ethics World

12 Lewis, L (2013) The outsider, *Prospect Magazine*, January

RESOURCES

The global efforts of researchers, companies, consultants, specialist bodies and government agencies continue to generate a rich resource on ethical leadership and cultures, their implications and challenges.

The downside of these valuable contributions is the effort needed to navigate this flood to reach the few precious islands of clarity and insight. This list of published resources is therefore highly selective.

Most busy executives lack the time to become immersed in what has become a tidal wave of literature. However, selectively using the resources listed here can deepen your understanding without trying to turn you into a world expert on ethics.

Alcatel-Lucent Sustainability Report (2011/2012) – an example of a comprehensive approach to running a responsible business, http://www.alcatel-lucent.com/sustainability/reports/Alcatel-Lucent-CR-Report-2011-EN.pdf

American Management Association/Human Resource Institute (2006) *The ethical enterprise: doing the right things in the right ways, today and tomorrow*, AMA, New York

Bibb, S (2010) *The Right Thing: An everyday guide to business ethics*, John Wiley & Sons, Chichester

Blue Rocket and The Good Folk (2009) The ethical business guide: how to run your business the right way, http://thegoodfolk.co.uk/The_Ethical_Business_Guide.pdf

Business Ethics: A manual for managing a responsible business enterprise in emerging market economies (2004) US Department of Commerce

Chartered Institute of Management Accountants (2010) Incorporating ethics into strategy: developing sustainable business models, Discussion paper, London, February

Collections of codes of ethics online: http://ethics.iit.edu/ecodes/ethics-area/5

Complete guide to ethics management: an ethics toolkit for managers, http://managementhelp.org/businessethics/ethics-guide.htm

Ethics Resource Center (2009) Ethics and employee engagement survey, Arlington, VA

Ethics Resource Center (2009) The importance of ethical culture: increasing trust and driving down risks, National Business Ethics Survey, Arlington, VA

Ethics Resource Center (2012) National Business Ethics Survey of Fortune 500 Employees: An investigation into the state of ethics at America's most powerful companies, Arlington, VA

Ethics resources online: http://www.vanderbilt.edu/CenterforEthics/resources.html

Ethisphere (2011) Best practices, leading trends & expectations of the world's most ethical companies, New York

Ferrell, OC, Fraedrich, J and Ferrell, L (2011) *Business Ethics: Ethical decision making and cases*, 8th edn, South-Western Cengage Learning, Mason, OH

Gebler, D (2005) Is your culture a risk factor? Working Values, http://accounting.smartpros.com/x49771.xml

Institute of Business Ethics (2012) An ethics policy and programme – what are they for?, http://www.ibe.org.uk/index.asp?upid=58&msid=11

Institute of Business Ethics (2012) Ethical dilemmas and decision-making frameworks, http://www.ibe.org.uk/index.asp?upid=86&msid=67

Johnson, CE (2012) *Meeting the Ethical Challenges of Leadership*, 4th edn, Sage, Thousand Oaks, CA

Lockheed Martin (nd) Integrity Minute Archive: short videos bringing to life real ethical dilemmas, http://www.lockheedmartin.com/us/who-we-are/ethics/iminute/archive.html

LRN (2012) The HOW Report: New metrics for a new reality: rethinking the source of resiliency, innovation, and growth, LRN, New York

Mitchell, J (2001) *The Ethical Advantage: Why ethical leadership is good for business*, Center for Ethical Business Cultures, Minneapolis, MN

National Center for Ethics in Health Care (2011) Ethical leadership: fostering an ethical environment & culture, Washington, DC

Prudential Financial, Inc (2012) Prudential's code of conduct: making the right choices, Newark, NJ, http://www.prudential.com/media/managed/MakingTheRightChoices.pdf

PwC (2010) Trust: the behavioural challenge, PwC Point of View, London, http://www.pwcwebcast.co.uk/dpliv_mu/Trust_the behavioural challenge_Oct 2010.pdf

Sample codes of ethics for selected companies and industries: Illinois Institute of Technology Center for the Study of Ethics in the Professions, http://ethics.iit.edu/research/codes-ethics-collection

Schein, E (2009) *The Corporate Culture Survival Guide*, Jossey-Bass, San Francisco

Seligson, AL and Choi, L (2006) Critical elements of an organizational ethical culture, Report, Ethics Resource Center, Washington, DC

Steare, R and Stamboulides, P (2008) Who's doing the right thing? Moral DNA Report, Roger Steare Consulting, Sevenoaks

Stoerger, S (nd) Business Ethics (website of useful resources), http://www.web-miner.com/busethics.htm

Sullivan, J (2009) The moral compass of companies: business ethics and corporate governance as anti-corruption tools, International Finance Corporation, Washington, DC

Thomas, T *et al* (2004) Strategic leadership of ethical behaviour in business, *Academy of Management Executive*, **18** (2)

Treviño, L and Nelson, K (2011) *Managing Business Ethics: Straight talk about how to do it right*, 5th edn, John Wiley & Sons, Inc, Hoboken, NJ

US Department of Commerce (2004) Business ethics: a manual for managing a responsible business enterprise in emerging market economies, http://ita.doc.gov/goodgovernance/adobe/bem_manual.pdf

Webley, S (2003) *Developing a Code of Business Ethics: A guide to best practice*, Institute of Business Ethics, London

World's Most Ethical Companies methodology: http://ethisphere.com/worlds-most-ethical-companies-methodology/

THE ETHICAL LEADERSHIP LITMUS TEST

Here is a Litmus Test to help you assess how ethical you are as a leader. The test measures leadership behaviours concerned with ethics at work, such as: having a strong voice (eg you constantly talk about core values and use them to guide ethical decisions); insight (eg you are socially aware); integrity (eg you make sure people at work are valued and treated fairly); and courage (eg you stand up for what is ethically right, even when others disagree).

Look at the statements below. Write next to each one the number that that most closely describes how much you agree with it, where 5 indicates you strongly agree with the statement, and 1 indicates that you strongly disagree.

1 At work, I constantly talk about and use core values to guide ethical actions and decisions. ☐

2 I help set the ethical tone by regularly explaining ethical values and the expected behaviours. ☐

3 I make sure people realize ethics are a priority and insist they treat them that way. ☐

4 I set high ethical standards and develop ways to hold people accountable for them. ☐

5 I stay alert to the impact of ethical issues and try to help protect the wider community. ☐

6 I assist others in dealing with ethical dilemmas in a sensitive way. ☐

7 I ensure we have a viable ethical plan for affecting behaviour at the corporate and individual levels. ☐

8 I keep looking ahead for what it means to be a responsible organization. ☐

9 I actively try to ensure those around me are valued and treated fairly. ☐

10 I try to ensure ethics influence all our decision making. ☐

11 I aim to do what is ethically right, not just to do it right. ☐

12 How we get results matters even more than what the results are. ☐

13 I will always stand up for what is ethically right, even when others disagree. ☐

14 Despite the obstacles I keep supporting our ethical programme. ☐

15 I seek to influence the long- and short-term ethical impact on individuals and groups of what we do. ☐

16 I am concerned how people feel, especially when it comes to ethical issues. ☐

17 I believe ethical issues are difficult and need judgement to resolve. ☐

18 I actively encourage people to raise ethical concerns. ☐

19 When people raise ethical issues I try to understand their particular concerns. ☐

20 I make sure people are rewarded for speaking up about ethical concerns, rather than punished for doing so. ☐

Ethical Leadership Litmus Test (LT) scoring

Maximum score possible = 100

Minimum score possible = 20

LT SCORE 81+ = STRONG Litmus Test Score

You are extremely ethical as a leader, and have much to offer to those around you.

LT SCORE 41 to 80 = MEDIUM Litmus Test Score

You are aware of ethical issues but could be more active in pursuing them.

LT SCORE 40 or UNDER = WEAK Litmus Test Score

You find it difficult making sense of ethics at work and would gain from additional help to become more aware and proactive.

Whatever your score, there is nearly always more you can do! Use your LT result to help you decide how best to proceed. In particular, review some of the many actions described in *Ethical Leadership*.

You can also try a slightly more challenging version of the Litmus Test and receive an instant score and question-by-question explanations at **www.ethical-leadership.co.uk**

© Maynard Leigh Associates 2013

INDEX